The

ROLE OF THE
LAND GRANT

The
ROLE OF THE
LAND GRANT
in the Social Organization
and Social Processes of a
Spanish-American Village
in New Mexico

by

Olen E. Leonard

CALVIN HORN
PUBLISHER, INC.

ALBUQUERQUE, NEW MEXICO 87106

CALVIN HORN, PUBLISHER, INC.
Albuquerque, New Mexico

IV

ACKNOWLEDGEMENT

I wish to acknowledge my appreciation to Dr. Carl C. Taylor and Dr. Chas. P. Loomis, who first interested me in rural sociology and who made the field work for this study possible. To Professor T. Lynn Smith, Head of the Departments of Sociology and Rural Sociology of the Louisiana State University, I am particularly grateful. His ever patient encouragement and constructive criticisms are largely responsible for any merits this study may have.

Olen E. Leonard

V

PREFACE

MANY BOOKS are of passing interest only. Some have qualities that give them a more lasting value. And a few become more important with every year that goes by. Leonard's penetrating study of the role of the land grant in the changing way of life of the people in New Mexico's small agricultural villages belongs in the third of these categories. Written a full quarter of a century "before its time", in a period when the social studies done in New Mexico had " all but ignored the highly important factor of the land" (p. 7), presently the volume is eminently germane to the pressing problems that are convulsing life in New Mexico and some of its neighboring states.

In many ways this small monograph illustrates the essentials of what even today may be considered to be the most valid and fruitful type of truly scientific sociological research. Its young, vigorous, and highly perceptive author took the time to master a comprehensive frame of reference through hard years of intensive graduate study. Likewise, in graduate school he familiarized himself with the ways of collecting and analyzing quantitative data and of perusing and evaluating materials contained in documentary sources. In the course of doing this he acquired a deep appreciation of the scientific attitude. He also gained command of the language (Spanish) he would need in mingling with and securing information from the villagers whose social institutions and way of life he was determined to understand. Then, through long months of residence in the community itself, he came to know intimately the social structures and social processes that characterized the little society in miniature; and while there he also made use of schedules of prepared questions to secure quantitative data pertaining to some of the more important features of the community's social organization and processes. Finally, he made a thorough search of archival and library materials bearing on the important subject he had chosen to study.

The pages of the monograph reveal unmistakably that many additional months were devoted to the work of analyzing, organizing, systematizing, and presenting the materials from the various sources in simple, clear, understandable language. The result of all this is a product whose interest and value are even greater today than they were when the study was completed more than a quarter of a century ago. Calvin Horn Publisher, Inc., is doing the world of learning a service by making conveniently available a new edition of one of the most significant studies ever made of a highly important part of New Mexican society.

T. Lynn Smith
University of Florida

TABLE OF CONTENTS

LIST OF ILLUSTRATIONS

XI

LIST OF TABLES

INTRODUCTION

W HY DOES a village become a ghost town? In some areas it is the lack of water, in other areas the mines are depleted. El Cerrito, like many other small villages located on land grants in northern New Mexico, became a ghost town for a reason hard to believe — the people lost their "common lands!"

The controversial decisions of the U.S. Court of Private Land Claims and the U.S. Supreme Court dating back to the 1890's, and the Homestead Act of 1916 which allowed people to file for homesteads on Public Domain, caused the villagers to lose their land.

The metes and bounds defining most of these grants were not clearly stated or easily identifiable. Many of the bounds were specified as a hill, a river, a tree or clump of trees (evidence of which has disappeared), or perhaps a rock or pile of stones which, in some cases, had long ago fallen down or been covered by sand.

The Spanish and Mexican laws supposedly limited these grants to eleven square leagues of land, or approximately 50,000 acres. Actually, many of the grants far exceeded this acreage. The particular grant under study here claimed 315,300 acres. Frank Blackmar in his book *Spanish Institutions of the Southwest* says: "the original holders of lands have lost most of their holdings either through misjudgements of the courts and commissions, or else by the wily intrigues of the Anglo-Americans, especially the latter. The Mexican

XV

has been no match for the invader in business thrift and property cunning."

Under Spanish and Mexican land grants the community type of grant, the type on which El Cerrito is located, contained two kinds of land — the irrigable land and the "common" or grazing lands for use of "rich and poor alike." There appears to have been few questions about the ownership of the irrigable land; but the grazing lands were the cause of much dispute between the grantees and the U.S. government. After much controversy and many years of delays the final survey was made in the months of December, 1902 and January, 1903 by the U.S. Deputy Surveyor, Wendell V. Hall, under contract 362 on "land reduced to actual possession and occupancy." The 5,024 acres assigned them out of the 315,300 in the original petition was distributed among the ten villages located on the original grant. Lime stone markers were set on all tracts. El Cerrito was allotted 117.65 acres.

Dr. Leonard discovered that, at the time the original grants were given and up to the time of the final U.S. Supreme Court decision in 1897, the people on this grant were not much concerned with who had title to the "common lands." These grazing lands had always been available for their use.

These people were unschooled in the laws of Private Land Claims, of Public Domain, and Patents, and did not understand what was taking place. Suddenly, they were forbidden to graze on lands they had once used freely; they could not so much as take firewood from areas where they had always obtained their supply of heat, and even more important they were denied easy access to much of their water supply. Adding insult to injury, these lands had been fenced! These people had never known fencing on their grazing lands.

Dr. Leonard says, "This decision was critical for El Cerrito and its inhabitants. Not only did they lose their land in this case, but much of their tangible and personal property was extended in an attempt to secure reversal of the Court's decision, only the irrigable land of the original grant was left to the people."

Thirty years ago Olen Leonard wrote this treatise, a vivid factual portrayal of the land grant problems and their effects on the Spanish-Americans in northern New Mexico. This sociological study was recorded long before the present stormy uprisings started.

El Cerrito, in western San Miguel County, was chosen for study because the life and the customs in El Cerrito were duplicated in most of the small Spanish-American villages in northern New Mexico.

Dr. Leonard lived in El Cerrito seven months while making this study. Knowing first-hand their problems, he said, "How much longer will they be able to hold out, unless relieved in some manner from the outside, is a problem confronting not only the Spanish-American people themselves, but every agency interested in the welfare of the area."

While Dr. Leonard was living there in 1940 there were 20 families comprising 136 people. Today, there are only two families consisting of six people. In approximately 30 years the population has declined about 95%. Thus, this small village was consigned to oblivion, a specter of its early days.

Come with me and visit this little village. After a

diligent search the back-country road to the village is found. The dust, which seems to have been waiting for someone to stir it up, engulfs everything. Meander down this seldom-used road until a fenced area with a sign on the gate "KEEP OUT" halts further progress. Today the grandson of the Aragon family stands guard by the gate. After an explanation of the mission, permission is granted to proceed toward the village.

Gradually, a descent is made down the dusty trail across the bridge over the Pecos River and into the little village in the hidden valley. A hush seems to have settled over the area. It must be *siesta* time. Stand in silence a moment absorbing the stillness broken only by a bird's beautiful song and the hum of the bee. Soon you realize what first appeared to be a sleepy little *adobe* village is only a group of *adobe* shells and tumble-down corrals and not a village at the *siesta* interval. Time and nature have combined to leave only traces of community life here.

The church with the bell intact, stands as a guardian over the village. A solemn reminder of a shy, self-reliant people who had to abandon their heritage in a short span of 30 years since this study was made, and 73 years since the U.S. Supreme Court decision. The neglected and forlorn looking cemetery has not had a burial in years and the graves are covered with weeds.

The small *adobe* homes, with mud plaster walls cracked or fallen to pieces, roofs collapsed, doors ajar or torn off, windows broken or shattered, are all sentinels of a past that is today only a memory. A barn still stands but the roof has caved-in. Beside the dilapidated barn stands a rack holding four horse collars seemingly ready to be used. Closer examination shows they have hung there many years, and sun and rain, snow and dust storms have all taken their toll. A mere touch and they would fall to pieces. Notice how the sheep corral stands at an angle. One push and it would tumble down.

A skeleton of a 1920 auto stands near a crumbling *adobe* house. A couple of the tires are missing while the remaining ones are rotted. The engine is gone, along with headlights and the windows. A basketball backboard, with its rim askew, still stands in the *plaza* as a reminder of ebullient youth of yesterday. Tumbleweed and wild squash have taken over the basketball court.

Amid these decaying ruins two families still struggle for livelihood, the Ferendes Quintanas and the Louis Aragons, both families descendants of the original grantees. Mr. and Mrs. Aragon talk with us and recall events of earlier days. Mrs. Aragon, now 82, was Estefanita Quintana. She remembered young Mr. Leonard when he lived there and has a copy of his book.

A village sunk in oblivion, and recorded in history as appeal case No. 25, U.S. Court of Private Land Claims, seems to sink deeper into the valley and the past as we ascend the road back to modern-day life.

After leaving this ghost town I read opinions and stories about the loss of lands to various other grants and such comments as: "It is difficult to impose one system of laws on another system," and "U.S. adopted a rectangular system of land division while the Spanish used the river front and indefinite boundaries," did not satisfy me.

The legal records were searched and showed that the first petition for claim to the 315,300 acres known as the San Miguel del Bado Land Grant was filed March 18, 1857, by Faustin Baca y Ortiz. An explanation could not be found for lack of action as long as 22 years after the claim was filed. November 13, 1879, the Surveyor-General at Santa Fe submitted a petition to Congress recommending the entire grant be approved. In 1881 the Secretary of the Interior referred the claim, along with three others, to the Senate who in turn referred it to the Commission on Private Land Claims. The claim was referred back to the Surveyor-General in Santa Fe for re-examination and it was returned by him to the Secretary of the Interior without question of boundaries. The report states:" nearly the whole of the land claimed is in San Miguel County and embraces all cultivated and uncultivated lands of the settlements mentioned."

Finally, on May 13, 1887, the Acting Commissioner of the General Land Office in Washington, D. C., in his report to the 50th Congress, First Session, states: "I am of the opinion that the survey of this grant is grossly in excess of the quantity granted. I would respectfully suggest that in the event of the confirmation of this claim by Congress, it be limited to the extent of the land reduced to actual possession and occupancy, to be ascertained by additional evidence and survey."

In March, 1897, six years after the U.S. Court of Private Land Claims was established to handle all unsettled claims, case No. 25 U.S. *v* Sandoval was appealed to the U.S. Supreme Court and the plea was denied. The final decree of the Court states:

Decree in United States v Sandoval and others *is reversed, and the cause remanded that a decree may be entered in conformity with this opinion; and it is so ordered accordingly.*

In brief, the Court explained the decision as follows:

Under laws of the Indies lands not actually alloted to settlers remained the property of the King, to be disposed of by him or by those on whom he might confer that power; and as, at the date of the Treaty of Guadalupe Hidalgo, neither the municipalities nor the settlers within them, whose rights are the subject of controversy in these suits, could have demanded legal title of the former Government, the Court of Private Land Claims was not empowered to pass the title to either, but it is for the political department of the Government to deal with any equitable rights which may be involved.

At times some of the material in this book may seem repetitious. Little has been changed in this study in an effort to keep the original intent of the work.

We hope, in reprinting this book, to bring the reader a better insight into the land grant controversy and the heritage of the Spanish-American people living in northern New Mexico.

CALVIN HORN

I

INTRODUCTION

NATURE AND PURPOSE OF STUDY

THIS STUDY is an attempt to discover the extent and nature of the relationships between the Spanish and Mexican land grants of New Mexico and the social organization and processes of the people who live on the land. Since it is assumed that the present situation, as it exists in New Mexico, is a product of what has gone on in the past, the approach to the problem has been somewhat historical in that the more significant changes in the New Mexican land situation are described from the time of the early Spanish settlements to the present.

The main objectives of the study may be listed categorically as follows:

1. From available secondary sources to determine the original nature of the Spanish and Mexican land grants and something of the history of change in the nature of these grants from the time of first Spanish occupation to the present, with special emphasis upon New Mexico. It was assumed that this should involve such factors as: type of grants allowed, rules and regulations governing the granting of the lands, subsequent changes in these rules and regulations, the stability of tenure on the grants, and the effects of the impact of

1

change brought about by the acquisition of the territory by the United States in 1846.

2. Study the social organization and processes in a selected Spanish-American village situated on an original Spanish or Mexican land grant.

3. To bring together the knowledge gained in these first two steps in order to discover and demonstrate the ways in which the land grant has affected the social organization and social processes in the village studied.

SCOPE OF THE STUDY

The scope of this study is limited in its general aspects to the Spanish-American area of New Mexico in general, in its more specific phases to the Upper Pecos Watershed of the state, and in its most detailed particulars to the community of El Cerrito. The location of these geographical and cultural areas and the village of El Cerrito are shown in Figures 2 and 3. For a plan of the village of El Cerrito, which was studied intensively, see Figure 1.

Several criteria were selected for choosing the village for intensive study. They were:

1. It must be within the limits of the predominantly Spanish-speaking area of New Mexico.

2. It must be at some considerable distance from any city or town that might have tended to influence it unduly.

3. It must be situated on an existing or original Spanish or Mexican grant of land.

4. It must exhibit certain characteristics of the Spanish-American area in general, such as: limited

land holdings, a combination of the enterprises of farming and stock-raising, a heavy dependence upon outside wage work, and above all perhaps, evidence a retention of old Spanish custom and tradition. These were the criteria previously set up to determine the boundaries of the Spanish-American area.[1]

After careful scrutiny of many records in New Mexico and numerous contacts with a wide range of technicians and government officials in the state it was decided that the village of El Cerrito, located in San Miguel County, would be an adequate choice. Upon examination, this village was found to meet each of the criteria for selection mentioned in the paragraphs above.

The time interval covered by the study is roughly from 1794 to the present with special emphasis on the year 1940 when the survey data for El Cerrito were gathered. The author spent from February 1, 1940, to September 1 of the same year in the village. Several return visits were made during the year 1942 for the purpose of checking specific points and securing additional facts. Contacts with the village have been maintained, by means of correspondence, from 1942 until the present time, April 1943.

Although the bulk of the data gathered were supplied by the inhabitants of the village of El Cerrito, it is believed that the results may be projected with a reasonable degree of accuracy to include the Spanish-American area of the state in general, and the Upper Pecos Watershed in particular. This assumption is

---

[1]Soil Conservation Service, *San Miguel County Villages*, Albuquerque: U. S. Department of Agriculture, 1938; also Tewa Basin Study, 1939.

based on the fact that an unusually high degree of uniformity and cultural homogeneity exists throughout the Spanish-American area. The nature and degree of this uniformity is developed in detail in Chapter III.

METHODOLOGY

It was recognized in the early stages of development of this problem that, to secure an adequate working knowledge of the social organization and processes of a village in the area, it would be necessary to go into the village for first-hand observation. At the time the village was selected for study it was expected that it would be possible to live in the village for a period of 12 months or long enough to observe the cycle of life and activities in the village over a full year. The actual time spent in the village was approximately seven months. During this period many hours were spent talking with these people, becoming acquainted with their attitudes, collecting data about their opinions and recording their case histories.

In order to gain admittance to the life of the village it was necessary to assume a role that would be accepted by the villagers. This proved to be easier than it first appeared. Upon arriving to live in the village every effort was made to distribute the information that I was "writing a history" of the village. This proved to be a popular role as most of the people are extremely proud of their history and are eager and willing to talk about it.

Although the approach to this problem is not primarily statistical certain figures and estimates were gathered on such factors as: size of holdings, ownership of land, value of possessions, etc. These figures were gathered by means of a small schedule which was completed for each family in the village.

Other sources of primary data were interviews with the "old timers" in other villages in the area, with governmental officials in the town of Las Vegas, and with the priests and sisters of the Catholic church in the area. Especially informative and interesting data were secured from the priest who serves the village of El Cerrito, a native Spaniard who has been in this country only a few years.

After primary data of these types were secured the next step was to assemble the data that would reveal the nature of the Spanish and Mexican land grants and their history. This involved intensive work upon the reports of the Public Land Office, reports of the Surveyor General, and other works on the Public Domain.

In analyzing the data of the study the fundamental objective has been to discover the role played by the Spanish and Mexican land grant as a conditioning factor on the social organization and processes of the village studied.

REVIEW OF SELECTED LITERATURE

There is a paucity of literature dealing directly with the subject. The bulk of the early records such as petitions for and grants of land were destroyed in 1680 when the Indians of New Mexico revolted and drove the Spanish from the territory. As a result the present sources of reference are of a very general nature such as: reports of the Surveyor General to the Public

Land Office from 1854 to 1891, special reports of the Court of Private Land Claims from 1891 to 1905, and a limited number of individual compilations of special data.

The Sociology of Rural Life by Smith provided the orientation for this study, especially parts III and IV which deal with rural social organization and the social processes of rural society.[2] The bibliography included in the volume was also useful.

The Systematic Source Book in Rural Sociology by Sorokin, Zimmerman, and Galpin was also a valuable aid in gaining a general perspective of social organization and the social processes.[3] Part two of Volume I was particularly helpful in its treatment of the ecology of the rural habitat.

Of the literature dealing specifically with New Mexico the *Public Domain* by Thomas Donaldson deserves special mention.[4] The some 1300 pages of this volume deal with the public land system and policies in all their ramifications. This document is by far the most complete and helpful of any yet published on the land situation, its nature and history, in New Mexico.

Another rich source of information was the files and miscellaneous unpublished reports of the Soil

---

[2]T. Lynn Smith, *The Sociology of Rural Life,* New York: Harper and Brothers, 1940.

[3]Pitirim A. Sorokin, Carle C. Zimmerman, and C. J. Galpin, *A Systematic Source Book in Rural Sociology*, Minneapolis: The University of Minnesota Press, 1930-32, 3 vols.

[4]Thomas Donaldson, *The Public Domain,* House Miscellaneous Document 45, 47th Congress, 2nd session, XIX. Washington: The Government Printing Office, 1884.

Conservation Service in Albuquerque.[5] During the period 1936-39 the Division of Human Surveys of the Soil Conservation Service made many surveys in the Spanish-speaking areas of New Mexico, revealing an abundance of information on land grants in the area. The recency of these surveys plus the wide range of data covered, make them one of the most valuable compilations of secondary data on Spanish-American life and conditions ever assembled.

Blackmar's *Spanish Institutions of the Southwest* has proven to be a reliable source of information on the early social and institutional life of New Mexico.[6] The extremely limited materials published on the subject make this book a classic in its contribution to the field with which it deals. Some of the other less complete works on the subject are: Adams' *History, Politics, and Education,* Dunham's *Government Handout,* Sanchez's *Forgotten People,* and Grisham's *El Pueblo.* Other sources on the subject are limited to casual and infrequent observations from works dealing with problems of another nature.[7]

---

[5] Soil Conservation Service, United States Department of Agriculture, Albuquerque, New Mexico. Some of the more pertinent studies are (1) *The Tewa Basin Study,* 1939, (2) *San Miguel County Villages,* 1938, (3) *Village Livelihood in the Upper Rio Grande Area,* 1937, (4) *Notes on Community Owned Land Grants in New Mexico,* 1937, and (5) *The Partido System,* 1939.

[6] Frank W. Blackmar, *Spanish Institutions of the Southwest,* Baltimore: The Johns Hopkins Press, 1891.

[7] Herbert B. Adams (editor), *History, Politics,* and *Education,* Baltimore: The Johns Hopkins Press, 1890, vol. VIII.

Harold H. Dunham, *Government Handout,* Ann Arbor: Edwards Brothers, Inc., 1941.

George I. Sanchez, *Forgotten People,* Albuquerque: University of New Mexico Press, 1940.

Glen Grisham, *El Pueblo* (unpublished), The Farm Security Administration, Amarillo, 1939.

On the history of the land grants of New Mexico alone there is no source of information that equals the records of the Public Land Office in Santa Fe, New Mexico. In the files of this office there are dockets containing all available data, such as the original petitions, testimony before the Court of Private Land Claims, etc., of more than 300 grants. Unfortunately, many of these dockets are incomplete because of the large incidence of loss of the old Spanish records.

For literature dealing with the general history of New Mexico heavy reliance was placed on Twitchell's *Leading Facts of New Mexican History*.[8] This five volume work contains a great deal of material pertaining to the subject of this paper.

Another complete and readable history of New Mexico is Coan's *A History of New Mexico*.[9] This book contains not only a chronological listing of important New Mexican events but develops the sidelights of such events much more completely than the general run of historical documents. The chapter on Spanish and Mexican Land Grants (Chapter XXVI, Vol. I), although brief, contains a remarkable compilation of concise data on some of the more important land grants of the state.

New Mexico History and Civics by Bloom and Donnelly has made some contribution to the subject.[10] The first 250 pages of the book deal rather completely with certain phases of New Mexican history and are

---

[8]Ralph E. Twitchell, *Leading Facts of New Mexican History*, Cedar Rapids: Torch Press, 1911-12, 5 vols.
[9]Charles F. Coan, *A History of New Mexico*, New York: The American Historical Society, 1925.
[10]Lansing B. Bloom and Thomas C. Donnelly, *New Mexican History and Civics*, Albuquerque: The University of New Mexico Press, 1933.

replete with pertinent observations and notations. It also contains a large list of bibliographical references to more complete and original works.

Odum and Moore's *American Regionalism* contains an interesting chapter dealing with the basis for setting the Southwest apart as an especially well defined region. Other sections of the book deal with certain concepts and definitions used throughout this paper.[11]

For a comparison of the New Mexico situation with that in other Spanish-speaking groups Simpson's *The Ejido: Mexico's Way Out* offers some of the history of land-man relationships in the Republic of Mexico and a fairly complete analysis of the land situation and its social implications in present day Mexico.[12] McBride does something of the same order for Chile in his *Chile: Land and Society*.[13]

Other less elaborate works on the man-land situation in New Mexico are also limited. All but a few of the social studies which have been done in New Mexico have all but ignored the highly important factor of land.[14]

ORDER OF PROCEDURE

Chapter I treats of the general nature of the problem under study and a general survey of the pertinent literature on the subject.

[11]Howard W. Odum and Harry E. Moore, *American Regionalism*, New York: Henry Holt and Company, 1938.

[12]Eyler N. Simpson, *The Ejido: Mexico's Way Out*, Chapel Hill: The University of North Carolina Press, 1937.

[13]G. M. McBride, *Chile: Land and Society*, New York: American Geographical Society, Research Series 19, 1936.

[14]A few of the more pertinent bulletins and Journal articles on the Spanish-American situation in general are:

Chapter II is a compilation of data on the general characteristics of the area and its population. These data include available information on: (1) The Land, its topography, soil types, vegetative cover, and major streams; (2) The Climate, the amount and distribution of precipitation and its adequacy for crops, pasture, and timber; (3) The People, physical and cultural types in the area, their geographic and cultural origins, and something of their relationships and associations.

In Chapter III an attempt has been made to point out the important factors which have gone into the making of what is referred to herein as "Spanish-American culture." Following this is a discussion of the nature, distribution, and development of this culture together with a review of the elements which illustrate how the village of El Cerrito is typical of this culture.

In Chapter IV a rather detailed description is

(Footnotes Cont.)

(1) C. P. Loomis, *Informal Groupings in a Spanish-American Village* (mimeograph bulletin), United States Department of Agriculture, Bureau of Agricultural Economics, 1940.

(2) Olen Leonard and C. P. Loomis, *Culture of a Contemporary Community, El Cerrito, New Mexico*, U. S. Department of Agriculture, Bureau of Agricultural Economics, 1941.

(3) Sigurd Johansen, "The Social Organization of Spanish-American Villages," *The Southwestern Social Science Quarterly*, vol. XXIII, 1942.

(4) Paul Walter, Jr., *A Study of Isolation and Social Change in Three Spanish-speaking Villages of New Mexico*, a Ph.D. thesis, Stanford, University, 1938.

(5) Florence R. Kluckhohn, *Los Atarquenos*, a Ph.D. thesis, Harvard University, 1942.

(6) Ernest E. Maes, "The World and the People of Cundiyo," U. S. Department of Agriculture, Bureau of Agricultural Economics, *Land Policy Review*, March, 1941.

(7) Kalervo Oberg "Cultural Factors and Land-Use Planning in Cuba Valley, New Mexico," *Rural Sociology*, 1940.

(8) John C. Russell, "State Regionalism in New Mexico," *Social Forces*, 1937.

given of the social organization and processes of the village of El Cerrito. An intensive field study of this village furnishes the bulk of the primary data used to test the proposition of the paper.

In the fifth and final Chapter the proposition of this study is developed, namely, that the Spanish and Mexican land grant has been an important factor in the conditioning of the social organization and processes of the village. The procedure in this chapter has been to give a brief history of the status of land distribution in New Mexico, types of land grants in the area, the significant features of Spanish and Mexican colonization policy, and subsequently, the radical changes in the land situation brought about by occupation of the territory by the United States. With this as background there is presented a discussion of the effects of the land grant on the social organization, institutions, and social processes as found in the village studied.

CHAPTER

II

GENERAL CHARACTERISTICS OF THE AREA

THE VILLAGE of El Cerrito is situated in the east-central portion of northern New Mexico. It is approximately at the center of what is generally designated as the "Upper Pecos Watershed," an area drained by the northern section of the Pecos River. The northern boundaries of this watershed reach to the crest of the Sangre de Cristo Mountains in Mora County. From this point southward it fans out considerably taking in almost all the western half of San Miguel County, in which El Cerrito is situated, and portions of northern Torrance and Guadalupe Counties.

THE LAND

In general this area is one of high plateaus or mesas, snuggled close to nearby mountain ranges, valleys and arroyos. The population is normally clustered along the various water courses at elevations varying from 5,000 to 8,000 feet and the area is seldom occupied for more than a few spring and summer months when livestock is commonly pastured at these higher elevations.

The oldest and most extensive outcropping formations in this watershed are members of the Mississippian, Pennsylvanian, and Permian series. These series, comprising massive exposures of limestones and sand-stones, are the principal outcrops in the northern and central parts of the watershed. In the central and east-ern parts of the watershed, these series are overlain by alluviums of the Quaternary period.[1]

The main soil types of the Upper Pecos Watershed are of the Rough Stoney Land and Reeves groups. They are largely made up of light-brown calcareous topsoils which are shallow and often unsuitable for cultivation. Underneath these topsoils are the cal-careous, yellow-brown subsoils resting on caliche or limestone. The absorptive power of these soils is low to medium. They are usually shallow and subject to wind and water erosion, except at the higher altitudes, where the vegetation is sufficient to prevent it. Ex-amples of this erosion are obvious and numerous even in the alluvial soils of the narrow valleys. Soil con-servation practices are made difficult by the widely scattered holdings and the fact that the people have not been convinced of the value of such practices. Reports of studies completed and others in progress repeatedly point out that the depletion of the grass cover crop by over grazing has added tremendously to the flood damage along the Pecos River during the past two or three decades.[2]

The covering in the Upper Pecos Watershed is divided into the three vegetative types: timber, wood-land, and short grass. These three areas are well de-fined in the watershed. The timber type lies in the

---

[1]Unpublished data from the Soil Conservation Service, United States Department of Agriculture, Albuquerque, New Mexico, 1939.

[2]Soil Conservation Service, U.S. Department of Agriculture, Pecos River Watershed, Albuquerque (unpublished), 1939.

northern part of the watershed, the short grass area runs along the eastern boundary, and the woodland area, the largest of the group, is in the southwestern section of the watershed.

The timber type, which consists largely of pine, fir, spruce, and oak, is concentrated in the higher area which will range in elevation from 7,000 to 11,000 feet. The land is largely Federally owned. Here the grazing and logging operations have been well controlled and erosion is at a minimum. Where this land is privately owned, it is characterized by severe erosion, cutover lands, overgrazed range, and submarginal farming land.

The woodland type lies below the timber area between the elevations of 5,000 and 7,000 feet. Here the timber is Juniper, Pinon, Oak and Scrub Pine. Although somewhat spotted, the grass covering is sufficient for grazing cattle and sheep. Much of this land is privately owned and is characterized by severe erosion and overgrazing.

The short grass area is somewhat below the woodland in elevation. This land is largely rolling prairie, and is characterized by less severe erosion as a result of its heavier vegetative cover. Large cattle and sheep ranches have absorbed most of this land during recent years. Only a fraction of it is farmed.

The main stream of water in the area is the Pecos River which divides the watershed into two very nearly equal parts. This stream is fed largely by melting snow from the nearby mountain tops. Such sources assure an almost constant flow of water for the entire year. Into the Pecos River flow such minor streams as the

Gallinas River, and Tecolote Creek. These two latter streams cannot be depended upon for water during more than a fraction of the year.

The runoff of these streams is extremely rapid and serious damage may be done along their banks within a few hours after a heavy rain. The average fall for the Pecos River is 13.8 feet per mile. For the area of the Upper Watershed the fall averages 67 feet per mile.

THE CLIMATE

The Upper Pecos Watershed area, like the remainder of the state of New Mexico, is deficient in rainfall. The amount differs according to altitude. Stations placed over the area show a variation from above 33 inches at the highest station to a little above 15 inches at a lower station some distance from the mountains. The general average for the area, based on records of 15 stations, is approximately 16 inches.[3] Fortunately for agriculture in the area the distribution of this rainfall is such that the heaviest precipitation comes during the summer months when the need is greatest.

The people of the area have come to depend heavily on the snowfall in the nearby mountains to furnish needed water during the spring and summer. Snowfall is extremely heavy in the high mountains, ranging as high as 300 inches at the top of the Sangre de Cristo ridge.[4] This snow, in a normal year, will furnish water for the river over a greater portion of the spring and summer months.

---

[3]U.S. Department of Agriculture, *Climate and Man, 1941 Yearbook of Agriculture*, Washington: Government Printing Office, 1941, p. 1015.
[4]*Ibid.*, p. 190.

The general direction of the winds in the area, as well as for the state as a whole, is from the west or southwest unless influenced by local conditions. During the summer months these winds are usually moist which is largely the explanation of the concentration of the rainfall in this season. The velocity of these winds is relatively high, ranging up to 50 miles per hour. The low moisture content of these winds plus their high velocity results in a high rate of moisture evaporation during the warmer months which may reach as much as 100 inches annually from a free surface. This evaporation varies with altitude being much less as the higher altitudes are reached.[5]

The variation in temperature for the area is extreme, ranging from a high of 108 degrees F. to a low of −32 degrees F. over a period of 15 years. The winters are generally cold and long. The last killing frost is generally around the first of May and the first one in the fall around October 1. This allows for a growing season of approximately 155 days.

ECONOMIC BASES OF SUBSISTENCE

As a result of the above factors it is obvious that the physical environment of the area is not conducive to intensive agriculture. Inadequate precipitation alone prevents extensive growing of crops except in areas where irrigation is possible. Largely for this reason the bulk of agricultural production in the area is done in the small, irrigated valleys that may be irrigated from accompanying streams.

Crops that are grown away from the streams are

---

[5]*Ibid.*, p. 1024.

largely beans, (harvested dry), and a limited amount of wheat. These crops are usually able to mature within the short growing season and the average precipitation of approximately 16 inches is sufficient to grow them if distribution for a particular year is well spaced.

A much wider variety of crops can be grown on the irrigable land of the valleys. Although wheat and corn predominate there are also many other crops such as alfalfa, oats, cane and garden crops. These garden crops assume a role of importance to the local people that would be difficult to overemphasize. On a plot of land no more than ¼ acre in extent, an industrious family may easily grow enough chili peppers, beans, onions and other vegetables to supply their family during the spring and summer months.

Although intensive agriculture is necessarily limited in the area by the physical factors of soil, climate, and topography, stock raising is profitable and possible providing ample grazing land and water are available. The grass in the area is of a short, bunch variety that is exceedingly nutritious and despite the rather severe winters range livestock may be kept out on the plateau or mesa land throughout the winter months with a minimum of feeding and shelter.

Until approximately the beginning of the twentieth century the agricultural base of the area consisted of a combination of stock raising and irrigation farming. A few families in each village owned the livestock and the remainder worked for them by the day or month. All farmed their irrigable land in the valley for food to supplement cash income earned from the livestock enterprise.

Since early in the 1900's this pattern of livelihood has changed. Pasture lands, once so abundant, are no longer in the hands of the village people. None of the villages in the area now own or operate enough land and livestock to give employment to all their people. Where formerly there were a dozen men in a village owning thousands of sheep each there are now only two or three with a few hundred each.

With this change in the economic base of the area the people began to seek work outside the area. At the present time the men go as far as Utah and Wyoming to work in the sugar beet fields, to herd sheep, and to work in mines. It is not unusual for a man to be gone for six months or even a year without returning to his home and family who were left in the village. Thus the pattern has become one of irrigated farming and migratory wage work. The irrigable holdings furnish a substantial part of the family's food, and the wage work provides the cash for buying whatever else the family uses.

THE PEOPLE

The population of the Upper Pecos Watershed is predominantly of Spanish-American origin.[6] According to a recent estimate based largely on school enrollment, the people of San Miguel County, in which the village of El Cerrito is located, are approximately

---

[6]The term Spanish-American is used generally throughout the Southwest, and especially New Mexico, to identify a group of people whose basic language is Spanish, who are of mixed Spanish and Indian blood, and who have been in the area for several generations. The term Mexican is often used to denote the same group but, as a rule, New Mexicans reserve this term for a group more recently from Mexico and more nearly of Indian descent. Hereafter, this term will be used to denote all Spanish-speaking people in the area who are not identified definitely as Indian.

83 per cent of Spanish-American extraction.[7] The remainder of the population is Anglo.[8].

The first Spanish-Americans to settle in the Upper Pecos Watershed area arrived in 1794.[9] They came from the upper regions of the Rio Grande River, near where the city of Santa Fe, New Mexico, is situated. They migrated to settle a tract of land that had been granted to them by the Spanish government.

These early settlers were descendants of Spanish and Mexican immigrants who had come into New Mexico after the re-conquest of the territory by De Vargas in 1692. For the most part these settlers seem to have been farmers and stockmen as contrasted with their forefathers who were a heterogeneous lot of ex-soldiers, adventurers, and men of fortune to whom the crown of Spain was under one obligation or another.

In Mexico and New Mexico their Spanish forbears had already mixed with the Indian elements to a considerable extent. Today the racial characteristics of these people indicate that a vast majority of them have varying degrees of Indian blood in their veins. Just what are these proportions of mixed blood in the veins of the Spanish-Americans has long been a matter of debate. There are some who maintain that the Spanish element is greatly predominant, although nearly every-

---

[7] George I. Sanchez, *Forgotten People*, Albuquerque: The University of New Mexico Press, 1940, p. 30.

[8] This term is used generally in New Mexico to designate the group of people whose basic language is English. It will be used in this paper to indicate all who are not Spanish-American or Indian.

[9] Public Land Office, *Land Grant Dockets*, Santa Fe, New Mexico.

one admits that some admixture had taken place prior
to the migration from Mexico.[10]

A search through the records of two of the oldest
churches in the area failed to disclose any marriages between the Spanish-American and Indian peoples. This
finding was substantiated by the experience of an in-
vestigator of the Soil Conservation Service who found
that "within the memory of the oldest inhabitants (of
northern New Mexico) there has been, except for rare
instances, no intermarriage between the Indians of the
region and the Spanish-Americans."[11] Certainly the
fusion of races which produced the Spanish-Americans
took place some time in the past.

As is the general rule with native peoples and cultural elements, the Spanish-American population of
the Upper Pecos Watershed is concentrated in the rural areas, living in villages along the several streams of
water. The majority of these villages are relatively old,
all but a few of which were settled between the years
1800 and 1840.[12] These settlements were almost entirely in the Woodland and Timber areas of the Watershed where the combination of irrigation farming and
stock raising was most feasible.

The Anglo is relatively a newcomer in the area.
One of the first to come into the area to stay arrived in
1848.[13] He married a local Spanish-American girl and

---

[10]George I. Sanchez, *A Study of Spanish Speaking Children on Repeated
Tests, A Thesis*, Austin: University of Texas, 1931, pp. 10-13.

[11]Soil Conservation Service, *Tewa Basin Study*, Albuquerque: U. S. Department of Agriculture, 1939, II, ii.

[12]Charles F. Coan, *A History of New Mexico*, New York: The American
Historical Society, 1925, pp. 475-79.

[13]Harold H. Dunham, *Government Handout*, New York: Edwards
Brothers, Inc., 1941, p. 218.

later came into possession of a sizeable grant of land. Others who came into the area before 1900 were largely of an adventurous type, some of them working for local stockmen and others doing hunting and trading.

The majority of the Anglos now in the Upper Pecos Watershed area arrived after 1900. Some of them came to homestead the land which was slowly being surveyed and others moved in to buy land patented by both Spanish-American and Anglo families. These families settled in the short grass section of the area which has proven to be more adaptable to sheep and cattle raising. These families came from Texas, Oklahoma and Kansas; the majority from Texas where they had been able to sell their former holdings at a fair profit and move westward where more land was available and at a cheaper price.

The Anglo families did not follow the village pattern of settlement established by their predecessors. Instead, they settled in a widely dispersed pattern, often near the center of their lands. This pattern still prevails for them today. Although the Anglo farmers own a substantial portion of the better grass lands of San Miguel County, it is concentrated in a few hands. The Extension Agent of the county estimates (1940) that there are no more than 200 Anglo farmers in the entire county. The total population of the county is roughly not more than 3,000 most of whom live in the town of Las Vegas.

Contacts between the Anglos and Spanish-Americans are at a minimum. In the first place, the two groups are separated spatially, the Spanish-Americans living largely in the western two-thirds of the area and

Anglos in the eastern one-third. Even in the town of Las Vegas the two groups are separated by a river which divides the town into two very nearly equal parts. Most of the inter-group contacts are brought about through business interests such as buying and selling livestock, hiring out for work and, in the town of Las Vegas, through purchases at the stores which are largely owned by Anglo merchants.

Despite the inflexible barrier that separates these two groups of people in their social activities, there is little overt conflict between the two. Over a period of several decades a pattern of social adjustment has taken place, is generally recognized and observed, which results in little overt conflict.

CHAPTER

III

EL CERRITO AS A TYPE SITUATION

THE NATURE OF SPANISH-AMERICAN CULTURE
IN NEW MEXICO

THE SOUTHWEST has been characterized as "the least American of all the regions" of the continental United States.[1] One of the principal criteria for substantiating this characterization is the large number of Spanish-speaking people in the region. According to the 1940 Population Census of the United States, the state of Texas alone numbered more than 700,000 of these people in its total population. In the four states of Texas, Oklahoma, Arizona and New Mexico there were a total of 1,066,280.

In the state of New Mexico alone, there is a large proportion of the Spanish-speaking people who are often set apart from the others and, as has been indicated above, given the special designation of Spanish-American.[2] In broad terms the Spanish-Americans of the state are the long-time residents of the state, des-

---

[1]Howard W. Odum and Harry E. Moore, *American Regionalism,* New York: Henry Holt and Company, 1938, p. 594. Although California and Colorado are not included in Odum's definition of the Southwest these two states showed Spanish speaking populations of 416,140 and 92,540 respectively in 1940.

[2]The remainder of the Spanish speaking people of the state are usually designated as Mexican and henceforth will be identified here by this term.

cendants of the early Spanish and Mexican colonists, generally considered to have a relatively high percentage of Spanish blood, and many cultural characteristics that distinguish them from the Spanish speaking people of the Southwest as a whole.

Roughly, these Spanish-Americans are concentrated in the north-central part of the state, in the counties of Guadalupe, San Miguel, Mora, Taos, Rio Arriba, Sandoval, Valencia, and Socorro. To the people of the area, Mora county is the cultural center of the area. The remainder of the Spanish speaking people of New Mexico are concentrated in the southern counties of the state. Large numbers of these people are only recently out of Mexico and a large percentage of them drift back and forth across the border, the shifting about depending upon the availability of work in New Mexico and the price such work will demand.

The racial composition of the Spanish-American element in New Mexico is generally conceded to be much more Spanish than the Mexican element. Although the degree of Indian blood in the veins of these people has often been a subject of controversy, it seems reasonable to assume that their physical isolation from the rest of the world has been a contributing factor in preventing any further mixing after the people were once in the area. In addition to the Spanish and Indian elements that went into the present Spanish-American product there is some evidence to support an argument that early immigrants from the United States into the area also contributed some blood to the fusion. The observations of an American traveler in the area around 1860 led him to remark:

Ah! Brother Jonathan and Mr. John Bull, what becomes of your proud theory of the "extirpating Saxon" in these frontier villages? What language do these little mongrel jackanapes, these young Mexican Parthenia, speak—yours, or that of the renowned Sancho Panza? Perhaps you don't understand bad Spanish. Do these poor Mexican girls learn English? or do their paramours rather learn Spanish? . . . My brave and "enterprising" countrymen, know you not that these wretched villagers . . . are indebted for their very existence to the presence of less than a dozen of you?[3]

As a matter of observation it is extremely frequent that one can see a person in the Spanish-American area with blue eyes and light hair. Such a phenomenon in the remainder of the state is seldom found.

The religion of the Spanish-American people of New Mexico is almost 100 per cent Catholic. During the past half century some considerable converts have been made to the Protestant religions among the Spanish-speaking people generally, with the exception of the strictly Spanish-American element. These people are extremely devout in their religion, attend church frequently and pay the small dues which the church requires of them from time to time. The women, as a rule, are much more observant of the church's teachings than are the men.

The Spanish spoken by these people has been branded as archaic and often incorrect.[4] It is true that there are many differences between the language they speak and the Spanish spoken in the southern part of the state or in Mexico. For example, the form *trujo*

3Stephen Powers, *Afoot and Alone*, Hartford: The Columbian Book Company, 1872.

4Soil Conservation Service, *San Miguel County Villages*, Albuquerque, 1938, p. 6.

is generally used for *trajo* and many of their nouns are pronounced differently from that in other parts of the state and elsewhere. This situation may largely be attributed to the fact that little Spanish has been taught in the public schools since the occupation of the territory by the United States in 1846.

The illiteracy rate for the state of New Mexico is one of the highest in the nation. The United States Census of 1930 revealed that 13.3 per cent of the total population of the state could not read or write. A student of the area has recently observed that "the counties with the highest proportion of Spanish-speaking people tend to have the highest illiteracy rates."[5] This observation is applicable to the Spanish-American area which contains the counties with the highest proportion of Spanish-speaking people. The reasons for the high illiteracy rate in the French-speaking area of Louisiana, as pointed out by Smith, are also applicable to this area where "they have values and standards, plenty of them, but they are not the values and standards of their English speaking neighbors. In view of their many vicissitudes, it is not difficult to see why they have been slow in adopting Anglo-Saxon ways, including Anglo-Saxon schools; and this, in turn, accounts for the fact that so many of them are unable to read and write."[6]

The school system in the Spanish-American area of New Mexico is probably the poorest in the state.

---

[5]George I. Sanchez, *Forgotten People,* Albuquerque: The University of New Mexico Press, 1940, p. 29.

[6]T. Lynn Smith, *The Population of Louisiana: Its Composition and Changes,* Louisiana Agricultural Experiment Station Bulletin 293, Baton Rouge, 1937, p. 65.

Many special problems attend the operation of the schools in this area that do not obtain elsewhere in the state. As Sanchez has said, the Spanish-American children "come to school, not only without a word of English but without the environmental experience upon which school life is based. He (the child) cannot speak to the teacher and is unable to understand what goes on about him in the classroom. He finally submits to rote learning, parroting words and processes in self-defense. To him, school life is artificial. He submits to it during class hours, only partially digesting the information the teacher has tried to impart."[7]

The Spanish-American area of New Mexico is an area of villages and small farms. The village is usually patterned according to the design set down by the Crown during the time of Spanish domination.[8] The center of the town is always the *plaza,* a rectangular plot of ground varying in extent from one to three acres. The houses are built along the sides and ends of the rectangle facing the *plaza.* The houses are frequently observed to be in long adjoining rows. This phenomenon develops over a period of time by the practice of a son, when he marries, building his house on to the side of that of his parents. Sometimes these rows of houses will reach the entire length of the *plaza,* an indication of the extended age of the village proper. The church and school buildings may be built along the side of the *plaza* or else within the *plaza* itself. This latter practice has become quite common in the building of the more recent villages.

[7]Sanchez, *op. cit.,* pp. 31-32.

[8]Frank W. Blackmar, *Spanish Institutions of the Southwest,* Baltimore: The Johns Hopkins Press, 1891, p. 212.

28

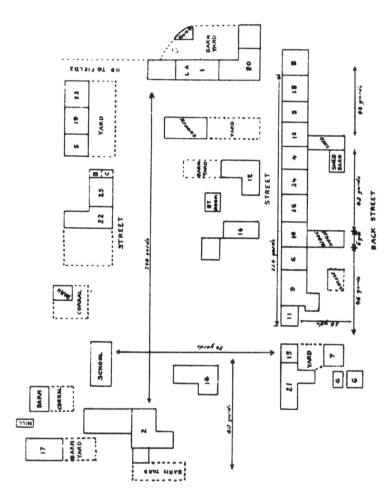

Figure 1. Location of Houses and Buildings, El Cerrito, New Mexico, 1940.

Behind the houses, and away from the *plaza,* are the barns, corrals, and sheds. See Figure 1. These facilities house the domestic livestock and the feed and grain stored for use during the winter months. Beyond the barns and corrals are the irrigated fields. These fields are usually quite close to the village, the distance depending upon the acreage of the valley floor. Still further away from the village, and on the mesa, are the dry farming lands and common pastures.

The house types in the Spanish-American area are remarkably uniform. The typical house differs from types in other parts of the state and area largely in its rather high, steeply pitched roofs, covered with sheet iron. House construction in the area is relatively good for the altitude is generally 6,000 feet or over and the winters severely cold. The walls are from 18 to 24 inches thick, and are of adobe (mud and straw) construction. Both the inside and outside of the walls are plastered with a thin sheet of mud. The ceiling is of thin cheese cloth or heavy paper. Doors and windows are purchased, except in a few villages where the doors are of heavy, thick timbers and elaborately carved. The floors are of wood or tightly packed earth.

The Spanish-American area of New Mexico is characterized by a high degree of farm ownership. The 1940 United States Census of Agriculture shows that in Taos County approximately 94 per cent of all farms in the county are owner operated. In the eight counties of Guadalupe, Mora, Sandoval, Socorro, Rio Arriba, Taos, Valencia, and San Miguel, in which the bulk of the Spanish-American population is found, only 10.8 per cent of the farms were tenant operated as compared with 17 per cent for the state as a whole. Thus the farmers of this area have clung to their holdings to an extent not achieved in other parts of the state. There seem to be two principal reasons for this. In the first place, these families have long been dependent upon their small, irrigated tracts of land to furnish a substantial part of their food. Secondly, there are no major and costly irrigation systems in the area to tax the land as has been the case on the lower Rio Grande and Pecos valleys.

The Spanish-American people of El Cerrito, New Mexico, have retained their Spanish social heritage to an extent not found in other parts of the nation. The chief form of amusement, namely dances, have been modified but little since the time of the early colonizations.[9] The modifications that have been made are mainly the results of increasing poverty in the area which has necessitated the cutting out of the many frills and fancy costumes, the conspicuous consumption, that were once in evidence. Now, as in 1800, the music for the dances is furnished by the guitar and violin. In fact these instruments are "seldom absent from any gathering and have an impartial place in most of the homes."[10]

Fiestas and other festivities are still celebrated at every appropriate occasion. All villages celebrate a two or three-day affair in honor of their "Patron Saint." This consists of church services, eating and drinking, speech making, followed by the inevitable *baile,* or dance. This celebration is held annually without ex-

[9]Blackmar, *op. cit.,* pp. 255-79.
[10]*Ibid.,* p. 258.

ception and is attended by everyone in the village; and any visitors that care to come are also welcome.

Holy Week is another occasion on which the villagers spend from three to five days in the observance of special ceremonies. Since this week is a specific church week the occasion is under the direction and supervision of the priest. Church services are attended from two to three times per day while the Holy Week is being observed; during the period there is much cooking and passing of food from one house to another. It is a time too when children who are away from home make effort to return to the village.

The Spanish-American area of New Mexico has come to be designated in other parts of the state as "Penitente Country." It is in this territory where the ancient art of flagellation is practiced in a number of villages during the Holy Week. At this time members of the order, who are Catholic, meet at a *morada* or meeting place away from the village, where they remain all week performing their rites. These are guarded by great secrecy. The climax of the ceremony is the "crucifixion" of an elected "Christ." Although the ordeal is still somewhat severe, the general opinion in the area seems to be that it has been modified somewhat during recent years. The church has long frowned on this order but with little avail. It still prevails in a large part of the area. "Penitente hunting" has become quite a popular sport for adventuresome Anglos during Holy Week, many of whom later express regret at having had such curiosity.

The Spanish-American has borrowed heavily from his Indian contemporaries in New Mexico, in making his physical adjustments to the area. He has learned a great deal from the Indian in the matter of crops, irrigation, and a multitude of minor techniques for dealing with the immediate environment.

In the matter of crops, the acquisition of *chili* (peppers) from the Indians was a valuable one. This *chili,* although extremely hot, is nutritious and grows readily on the irrigated soil of the area.[11] There are few Spanish-American families in northern New Mexico that do not serve *chili,* in one form or another, in at least two of the three meals of the day. It is eaten green, dry, powdered, and mixed with every sort of meat and vegetable. To deprive one of these families of its *chili* would be considered a crime of almost equal importance with depriving it of bread. Every house will contain one or more long strands of these pods, whose rich yellow and red colors add a highly decorative effect to the dwelling.

Another important Indian food used extensively by these people is the blue maize or Indian corn. It is grown exclusively for human consumption, being much preferred to other varieties. This corn, in the hands of a skilled Spanish-American housewife, can be turned into a wide variety of dishes ranging from hominy and meal to a number of choice desserts. *Tortillas, tamales* and other typical dishes of the area are generally considered to be of a much higher quality and taste if made with this type of corn.

---

[11]Arthur Goss, *Nutrition Investigations in New Mexico,* New Mexico Agricultural Experiment Station Bulletin 54, Las Cruces, 1898, Chapter 1.

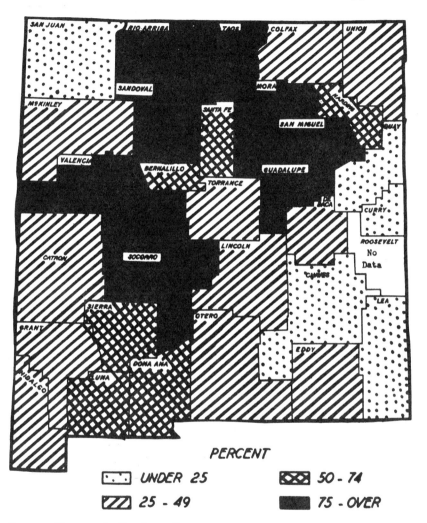

PERCENT

⋅∴ UNDER 25   ⧓⧓ 50 - 74

▨ 25 - 49   ■ 75 - OVER

Source: George I. Sanchez, *Forgotten People,* Albuquerque,
New Mexico, University of New Mexico Press, 1940.

Figure 2.   Percentage Distribution of Spanish-Speaking People of New Mexico, 1938.

THE DISTRIBUTION OF SPANISH-AMERICAN
CULTURE IN NEW MEXICO

The Spanish-American population of New Mexico is concentrated in the north-central part of the state. In the group of ten counties surrounding the headwaters of the Rio Grande River live 170,000 of these people.[12] This is approximately 1/3 of the state's total population, and a little less than 80 per cent of the total Spanish-speaking people of the state. In all but two of these ten counties the percentage of the total population which was Spanish-American is over 75. See Figure 2. In Mora, Taos, and Rio Arriba counties the percentage was over 90. See Table I. For the area as a whole, in 1938, all but 25 per cent of the population was Spanish-speaking.

TABLE I

SPANISH-SPEAKING POPULATION OF CERTAIN SELECTED
COUNTIES OF NEW MEXICO, IN 1938

County	Number	Per cent of Total	County	Number	Per cent of Total
Guadalupe	7,161	85	Socorro	10,645	78
San Miguel	24,992	83	Valencia	15,772	81
Mora	10,899	96	Bernalillo	35,202	53
Taos	14,229	93	Santa Fe	15,784	67
Sandoval	12,070	83	Rio Arriba	23,383	93
Total	170,137	75			
				Totals	Totals

Source: School enrollments, growth of school census, and 1930 U.S. Census of Population, from Sanchez, *op. cit.*

With the exception of the urban populations of Albuquerque, Las Vegas, and Santa Fe these people are clustered in small villages along the upper Pecos and Rio Grande Rivers and their tributaries. See Fig-

---

12George I. Sanchez, *Forgotten People,* op. cit., p. 30, Counties Guadalupe, San Miguel, Mora, Taos, Sandoval, Socorro, Valencia, Bernalillo, Santa Fe, and Rio Arriba.

ures 2 and 3. Thus, in brief, the total Spanish-American population of New Mexico, with the exception of a few widely separated villages, is concentrated within a fifty mile radius of the city of Santa Fe.

THE DEVELOPMENT OF SPANISH-AMERICAN CULTURE IN NEW MEXICO

The first Spanish colonizing party of any permanence crossed the Rio Grande in 1598. This party was led by Don Christobal de Oñate and consisted of 400 persons.[13] After a slow and laborious journey of approximately three months the party reached the junction of the Chama with the Rio Grande River where is situated the Indian Pueblo of San Juan.

These colonists appear to have been a motley set of adventurers and men of fortune. Available records indicate that "the colonists were not farmers and down to the summer of 1608, even with the help of the laboring class, they did not 'make a crop' which was adequate to their needs."[14] As a result they lived off what they could secure from the Pueblo Indians of the vicinity.

Colonization of New Mexico in the seventeenth century made but little progress. However, there is evidence that the present town of Santa Fe was settled during this period and also the village of San Gabriel. The total population of the present state of New Mexico was only 2,000 at the end of the century.[15]

---

[13]Coan, *op. cit.*, p. 175.
[14]Lansing B. Bloom and Thomas C. Donnelly, *New Mexico History and Civics*, Albuquerque, University of New Mexico Press, 1933, p. 83.
[15]Coan, *op. cit.*, p. 184.

Although considerable effort was expended by the Spanish government in inducing settlers to move into the territory of New Mexico during the 18th century, such efforts seem to have had little result. The ill fortunes of the earlier colonists in the territory, plus the fright caused by the pueblo revolt of 1680, discouraged extensive settlements during the century. The largest number of Spanish people in the territory, between 1700 and 1800 was 23,769 if the figures of the many Spanish censuses may be relied upon. The Spanish populations of New Mexico, for certain years, during the century were given as follows.[16].

Year	Population	Year	Population
1700	2,000	1794	17,330
1750	5,179	1799	23,769
1766	10,524	1805	26,835

During the Mexican regime in New Mexico, from 1822 to 1846, the rate of settlement in the territory speeded up somewhat. By this time the American colonists had crossed the Allegheny Mountains and were moving westward at a rate that alarmed Mexican officials. As a result, the Mexican government made every effort to establish additional colonies in the territory of New Spain. The result of these efforts may be seen in the following figures for the "Mexican" population in the territory from 1822 to 1845:[17]

It is interesting to note that all of the Spanish-speaking people (exclusive of Indian) in the present

Year	Population	Year	Population
1822	30,000	1833	57,176
1827	43,433	1845	67,736

[16]Ibid., pp. 238, 257, 281, 325.
[17]Ibid., p. 325.

37

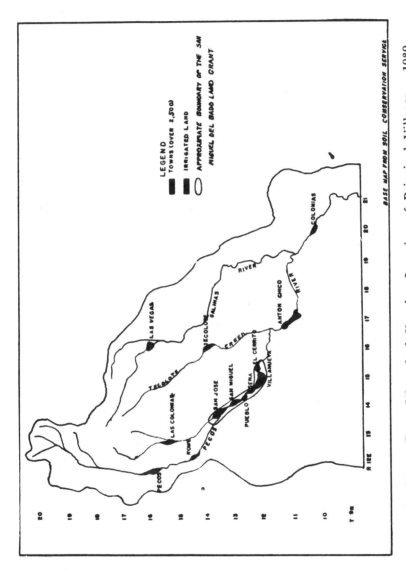

Figure 3. Upper Pecos Watershed Showing Location of Principal Villages — 1939.

state of New Mexico who were in the area at the time of American occupation in 1846 were living in what has been designated in this paper as the Spanish-American area. A map of the inhabited places in New Mexico in 1844 shows the Spanish-speaking population as concentrated in an area within fifty mile radius of the present town of Santa Fe or at the headwaters of the Rio Grande and Pecos Rivers.[18]

With the occupation of the territory of New Mexico by the United States government in 1846 and the establishment of the international boundary between the United States and Mexico in 1848 (treaty of Guadalupe Hidalgo) a n d 1853 (Gadsden Purchase) the Spanish-American area became virtually isolated from the rest of the world. Contacts with other people of the United States were limited to those with various trading expeditions that came into the area from time to time and with Mexico, to the itinerant stragglers that drifted across the boundary at intervals in search of work. By and large, however, the immigrants from Mexico remained in the southern parts of the state, in the Lower Pecos and Rio Grande Valleys. As a result the southern part of the state remained under the cultural influence of the Mexicans, with its subsequent changes, while the people in the northern part of the state retained much more nearly the culture they had brought from Spain. This, with what they learned and adopted from the Indians, blended into a pattern that has come to be recognized at least in New Mexico, if not the Southwest, as Spanish-American culture.

---

[18]*Ibid.*, p. 305.

THE UPPER PECOS WATERSHED AS A SPECIAL AREA

Within the larger Spanish-American area of New Mexico certain special or sub-areas may be delimited. One of these is the drainage basin of the Upper Pecos River. This sub-area contains parts of the counties of Mora, Santa Fe, San Miguel, Torrance, and Guadalupe. It begins at the headwaters of the Pecos River, in Mora County, and extends southward to a point just below the junction of the Gallinas with the Pecos River. See Figure 3.

This area totals approximately 1,800,000 acres about 35,000 of which are farmed. Half the total area is contained in large land grants that, until fairly recently, were community owned. Now, however, these grants are largely in the hands of private, nonresident livestock operators. Only about 130,000 acres are now in the hands of villages or communities.[19]

In this area lives a group of people who are homogeneous to a remarkable degree. Almost the entire Spanish-speaking people of the area can trace their ancestry back to the first group of settlers who came into the area just before 1800. These communities are geographically isolated from the rest of the state by high mountains on the north and west and by long stretches of semi-desert country to the east and south. Until modern roads were built through the area since 1900 it was a trek of several difficult days to reach Santa Fe, the nearest city on the outside, a distance of approximately 50 miles by the most direct route. This made contacts with other parts of the state very dif-

---

[19]Soil Conservation Service, *Upper Pecos Project* (unpublished), Albuquerque, 1939, p. 2.

ficult and occasions not enjoyed by a family more than once or twice during the year.

Originally this was the area of the largest livestock enterprises in the state, where one or two men from each village could number their livestock in thousands. Today, it has suffered more, perhaps, than any other area of the state from loss of pasture and grazing lands because of the originally heavy dependence u p o n sheep. As a student of the area has expressed it "though they did farm the narrow valleys, their hope of economic advancement and prosperity was based upon stockraising."[20] While most of the villages in the Spanish-American area have retained enough irrigable land to provide some cash crops the sub-area of the Upper Pecos Watershed has come to depend almost entirely on outside employment to provide the cash for their family living.

The old Spanish *fiestas, bailes* and other activities are carried on in this area to an extent not practiced any more in the Spanish-American area as a whole. Physical isolation from the outside world has prevented their contacts with other people and hence has served to retard change to a greater extent than is true of the other sub-areas of the region.

These people are also set apart from the remainder of the Spanish-American area in the thinking of the group and the other Spanish-Americans outside. They are often referred to as *los Manos* or people of the mountains. They often refer to themselves as *los pobres* or the poor people of New Mexico.

---

[20]Glenn Grisham, *El Pueblo* (unpublished), Amarillo: The Farm Security Administration, 1939, p. 4.

EL CERRITO AS A TYPE SITUATION

In a broad sense, the people in the village of El Cerrito are a part of the 1,574,960 Spanish-speaking people reported as living in the six states of Oklahoma, Texas, Colorado, New Mexico, Arizona, and California in 1940.[21] This entire group of people may be identified in so far as they: speak the same language, have somewhat the same physical characteristics, share something of a common tradition, and are usually identified by non Spanish-speaking peoples as "Mexican."

The village of El Cerrito is identified much more closely, however, with some 170,000 Spanish-speaking people concentrated in north-central New Mexico and designated in this paper as Spanish-American. For the people of El Cerrito are Spanish-American in each of the number of characteristics used to describe the Spanish-American culture on previous pages.

Most specifically, however, El Cerrito is a definite segment of the Spanish-American sub-area previously designated as the Upper Pecos Watershed. It is very probable that nowhere in the continental United States could one find an area that is more homogeneous in people, culture, occupation, and general well-being.

Of the some sixty villages in the area one could hardly find any social phenomenon in any one of them that could not be duplicated in each of the others. The physical appearance of these villages is the same with only minor variation except for size which may vary from a population of 20 to 200. The land holdings in each of the villages are small in size, ranging from

_____

21United States Census of Population, *Bureau of the Census*, Series p-15, No. 1.

$\frac{1}{4}$ to 20 acres. In none of the villages is the extent of available land sufficient to care for the needs of the resident families. Wage work on the outside has come to be almost the sole source of cash income for all but a few families which have been able to maintain small herds of cattle or sheep.

Thus by examining in detail the social structure and processes of any one of the village units in the area, such as El Cerrito, it is possible to learn much about the general nature of society in the entire Upper Pecos Watershed. By examining only one small community, on the other hand, it is possible to go into much greater detail than if an attempt were made to include the entire area.

IV

CHARACTERISTICS AND DESCRIPTION OF EL CERRITO[1]

DESCRIPTION

THE VILLAGE of El Cerrito is located on the Pecos River in one of the many land pockets formed at irregular intervals where the valley has widened out sufficiently to allow for a few houses and a little irrigable land. There is nothing singular about the village of El Cerrito in the area in which it is situated. Rather it is extremely similar to a large number of others in the vicinity. As pointed out in Chapter III it is only one of a large number of villages where the people live in the same type of houses, practice the same manners, customs and mores, speak the same language, and have an identical cultural heritage.

The village of El Cerrito is 30 miles southwest of the town of Las Vegas. Sixteen of these miles are over first-class pavement, three over a semi-improved surface, and the remainder over only a very rough and often-changed entrance to the village itself. It is well

---

[1]A part of this study has been published previously as: Olen Leonard and C. P. Loomis, *Culture of a Contemporary Rural Community*, El Cerrito, New Mexico, Rural Life Studies: I, Washington: U.S. Department of Agriculture, 1941. Parts of this publication reproduced here are either exclusively the work of the author or else are given special mention.

hidden from the outside world. Only one familiar with the area or equipped with detailed instructions would be able to find it without patient searching or striking good fortune. One comes upon the village suddenly if in a car. Driving over the high mesa covered with juniper and scrub pine, one finds the road rising abruptly, then turning sharply to the right, where a panoramic view of the entire village and valley is sighted. Still over a mile beyond and below, the houses stand out in quiet relief against the far side of the valley wall. The miniature fields stretch out in rectangular fashion, clearly bounded by stretches of rock or the more modern barbed wire fence. Approached in winter the village seems as quiet and lifeless as the little cemetery just above it.

As one approaches still closer to the cluster of houses, almost the full length of the little irrigation ditch that brings the water from the river to the homes and fields can be seen. This ditch is an engineering feat done without the aid or benefit of modern science. Its style of construction and the height of its banks built by annual cleanings give ample testimony of its age. It is said to have been built by the Indians, predecessors of the present inhabitants of the village, many years before the Spanish settlers came into the region.

Driving on a little further one crosses a new and modern bridge on the Pecos River and enters the confines of the village. Although there are 136 people living in the village, if the driver is a stranger he is likely not to see more than a few stragglers, mostly children, in the streets. They are a shy people when strangers appear and prefer to stay inside their houses and peep through or around drawn curtains to meeting the stranger outright.

Once inside the *plaza* one is struck by the uniformity of the village. From the center of the *plaza* one can count every house in the village including the community buildings, the Church and the School. On one side of the *plaza* the houses are all attached together in the form of a long row. These houses are the property of the "Patron" family of the village and have become a long row as the result of the sons building onto the parent house when they married and moved to themselves.

The language the visitor will hear is Spanish for most of the residents speak no other. The children learn English, of a sort, in school, which is quickly and effectively forgotten within a few years time after they leave the school room.

HISTORY AND BACKGROUND

The date of the original occupancy of the village of El Cerrito goes back well over a century. One of the oldest residents of the village was born here and says that his grandfather came here when he was a young man. Practically all of the families are descendants of the pioneer settlers who moved onto the present site in order to be nearer their grazing lands. They came from neighboring villages, the majority from San Miguel which is the parent village of the San Miguel del Bado land grant on which the village of El Cerrito is located.

In the early days of settlement, cattle raising was

the principal economic enterprise, and the owners of the stock, by reason of their possessions, occupied positions of exalted importance in the community. Non-owners, and their families, depended heavily upon them for advice as well as employment. Such men accepted this responsibility and eventually came to dominate all the affairs of the village. Dependents and incapacitated persons came under their protection. Under a well-regulated and organized system, available work was distributed in accordance with need to those not regularly on the "Patron's payroll." The only independent economic pursuit of all laborers was the cultivation of their small irrigated land holdings. As the local irrigated land was "granted" land and as all families were descendants of the original grantees, each family was entitled to a small holding.

These early settlers in El Cerrito found the area especially adaptable to stock raising. Although the land on the mesa was poor for farming, it had a good covering of bunch grass. It was this abundant pasture land that induced the settlers to come to their new location. Part of the area had been in use by the people from San Miguel previously but its distance from the village had prevented their making full use of it.

Farming on land which could not be irrigated never offered a great deal of inducement in this area. A rigourous climate and scant rainfall are serious handicaps to much dry land farming. Rainfall is not only meager but extremely uncertain. Although the annual precipitation for this area ranges from 15 to 18 inches, half of this may come within a few days' time with no more for a period of weeks. There is usually sufficient moisture for planting of crops in May, but June is likely to be extremely dry, with rain again in July and August.[2] This is the expectation pattern under which the local farmers operate.

Despite the odds against such an enterprise many of the original settlers of El Cerrito undertook part-time, dry land farming on the mesa lands. Corn and wheat were the principal crops cultivated and for a time the new soil and favorable seasons combined to make such enterprises partially successful. But, within a brief span of time the majority of the families abandoned the practice in favor of the more certain jobs with local stockmen. Those who did continue to farm the mesa land did so on a substantially reduced scale.

Because of these environmental factors, dry land farming lasted only through an experimental stage. Only the irrigable land of the local valley proved its worth for intensive and continuous agriculture. This land was fertile and water from the Pecos River was always available. Hence the people became more and more dependent upon the products of their small irrigated holdings as a basic factor in their livelihood. Money and goods earned at wage work, plus the subsistence products grown at home enabled these families to survive in a satisfactory way. Both sources of income were of tremendous importance. The failure of either to contribute meant deprivation if not near destitution.

The early economy of El Cerrito seems to have been one of plenty. Land was available and could be

2Department of Agriculture, *Climate and Man, 1941 Yearbook of Agriculture,* Washington: Government Printing Office, pp. 1015-1024.

had for either the asking or the taking. Temporary depletion of the grass resource invoked little more hardship than moving livestock to another proximate area or spreading it over a wider base. Little thought was given to the fact that some day the soil might be impoverished or exhausted. On the other hand, some effort was made to preserve the soil of the valley. The practice of spreading barnyard manure on the soil seems to go back well into the history of the village of El Cerrito. During the last few decades the necessity for this practice has been increasingly realized.

Each of the two classes of land cultivated, dry and irrigated, had its own special crops that were planted year after year. The dry-farming land was devoted to wheat and some corn, the irrigated land to corn, alfalfa, and garden crops. There was little diversification. The same piece of land might be planted year after year to the same crop.

The village of El Cerrito is located on a part of the San Miguel del Bado land grant which o n c e claimed approximately 400,000 acres. Local residents place the turning point in their economic stability to the date 1904 when the U.S. Court of Private Land Claims denied to them all but 5,024 acres.[3] This decision was critical for El Cerrito and its inhabitants. Not only did the people lose their land in this case, but much of their tangible and personal property was expended in an attempt to secure a reversal of the court's

[3]Coan, op. cit., p. 478, also the records of the Public Land Office, Post Office Building, Santa Fe, New Mexico. These records carry the complete history of approximately 300 land grants up until a final decision in each case was made.

decision. Only the irrigable land of the original grant was left to the people.[4]

Although the people's grazing lands were legally taken from them by the court's decision in 1904, it was not for a number of years later that the loss was actually felt in all its harshness. In the interval wage work had been plentiful and at a price considerably higher than the sheep and cattle men could or would pay their employ. As a consequence land became of secondary importance with little thought of depending upon it for a livelihood when so much more might be earned at day labor with the railroad or in the mines.

This era of prosperity lasted well into the 1920's. However, by 1928 wage work was extremely difficult to procure and many of the migrant workers from El Cerrito began to debate the possibility of returning to the land. After 1930 little hope remained of obtaining outside employment and a wholesale retreat began back to the villages and the land. Although it was generally realized that the land situation had changed somewhat, the returning workers were hopeful that the situation was such that they might till their own irrigated holdings and run a few cattle or sheep on the mesa.

It was not until the families were again dependent on their land that full realization came as to what had happened during the wage work boom. Now all free or grazing land was gone. Large concerns had patented, bought, fenced, and posted huge areas, denying their

----

[4]El Cerrito was not the only village affected by this decision. A total of ten villages, including El Cerrito, were located on the original grant and were affected in like manner.

use to the villagers. It was even forbidden that the people should remove wood for fuel, a practice to which they had long been accustomed. See Plates. Many of the tracts of land still remaining in the possession of the villagers were now distributed in such a manner that their value for use was almost negligible. For example, a man from the village might own a section of land only two or three airline miles from the center, but because of new fences it might be necessary to travel ten miles to reach it. The homesteads that were more accessible were likely to be useless because of lack of access to water. The owners of the new holdings had been systematic in their program of securing control of water resources, for this, in turn, meant control of the surrounding land. In sum, the people suddenly realized that they had allowed themselves to be led into a situation from which there was no retreat. There was no longer any alternative but employment away from the village or aid from the outside.

The changes that have come about during the last half century in and around the village are told very vividly in the life history of the oldest inhabitant. It is given below as he unfolded it.

I was born in El Cerrito and have lived here all of my life except 2 or 3 years. These years were spent in other parts of New Mexico while I was working for the railroad and as a freighter. I owned a little property in El Cerrito all this time and thought of it (El Cerrito) as my home.

My father was a very strong and healthy man. I remember him very well as he lived to be 55 years old. He was born in Santa Fe. He used to tell us many stories of life in Santa Fe when he was a boy. The place was very tough then and there was always danger from the Indians. He used to fight the Indians and was a very good fighter, too.

When he was very young he came to Pecos (town in San Miguel County) and worked there for a long time. He then moved to San Miguel and it was there he met my mother and they were married. When they were married, he bought some land in El Cerrito and moved there. I was born here in 1862.

My father worked very hard and was a good business man. Soon after he came to El Cerrito he bought more land (in another village some 10 miles from El Cerrito) but most of his money went for cattle. He was very well off financially, had lots of money always. In a few years he had several hundred head of cattle. He used to keep money around the house in jars.

My father believed in working hard and he made us work hard too. He used to get up very early in the morning, while it was still dark. There were horses to feed and water to bring. A boy of 8 years then was expected to be able to work all day. We worked much harder than the boys do now. Oh, much harder. The girls worked, too, but it was for the man. The women had plenty to do around the house. There was wool to card and spin. There were clothes to make, too. We made most all of our clothes then. It was so much better than now when one has to buy everything. Money wasn't important then. Everything was made at home and not bought at a store.

Although we worked hard in those times, we used to find time for play. We could play on bad days, on Saturday afternoons, and Sunday after Rosary. We couldn't play before Rosary on Sunday. There were several games which we played. We used to take a ball and toss it to one another. Used to play a game something like golf. The balls were made by hand and so were the sticks.

My father didn't mind our playing as long as we did our work well. He would never join in with us but would often stand and watch us play for long periods of time.

When I was a boy many people would die and get killed.

There was much danger during those days. When a person died the custom was for all of the man's friends and relatives to visit the dead man's family. I didn't mind going to those places. There was always plenty of food to eat. However, I didn't like the burials. I used to get scared when they began to throw dirt on the body.

When I was a boy the Indians would come to the village at night. They would steal meat and lard from the houses. The people here always had meat and lard made from the buffalo. The Indians used to steal *tortillas* too. They would bring long pointed sticks and spear the *tortillas* from the windows.

One time the Indians came while my father was taking an ox to water. They took the ox away from him and ran up into the mountains. When father came back to the village, he ran to a huge drum in the village, used for warning the people against the Indians, and began beating on it. When the people heard the noise, they came and went after the Indians. They finally found the ox but there was nothing left but the bones. The Indians had killed the ox, cut off the meat, wrapped it in a *serape,* and gone away.

I went to school very little when I was a boy. The school term was short and we were taught in Spanish. Nothing more than the catechism and the letters were taught then. About all the teachers knew then was how to say A, B, C, etc.

I can remember those teachers very well. They were all men and were very mean to the children. They believed in using the whip freely. They used to make us cross our fingers, then they would tie the fingers together and whip us. They used small leather quirts. Sometimes they would make us take off our clothes before they began whipping us. I think everyone was too afraid of the teacher then to learn anything.

I can remember when the church sponsored lots of *fiestas* and dances. Those were good times when everyone had lots of fun. Sometimes the *fiestas* would last for several days. People would bring food and eat together.

When I was small a woman who was very rich lived here.

She made a lot of money from sheep and cattle. (A member of the rival family in the village.) She had several peons and was very mean to them. Used to have them lashed when they disobeyed her. She didn't get along very well with the people here. She would cheat them and pay them very little when they worked for her. I remember a foreman that used to work for her. He was a very mean but a very funny fellow. He was always playing jokes. He used to milk cows for her. I remember one time he milked a pail full from a cow and then sat in it. That was very funny.

Times were good then and everyone had some money. No one lacked food and there was always work. There was a system here then that has died out. The people in El Cerrito used to elect a *conservador* each year. He acted as a sort of governor of the village. The people had to do what he told them to. In those times the people would work together in planting and harvest time. The *conservador* would call the men to work and could determine which work should be done first. When someone wanted to hire a man he had to come to the *conservador*. He could determine who could have the job. Always he would select the family that needed the work most. In that way the needy were usually provided for. In case they were not, he could ask the people for money or grain to give the *pobres*. I don't think he ever had much trouble with the people—everyone did as he told them.

My family was very large. There were eight children, four girls and four boys. When my father died we were all living at home. He left the property to mother but the boys managed everything. We did this, dividing the profits equally. This continued until my mother died four years later. Then the property was divided into eight equal parts.

A few years after my mother died a man by the name of R. came to Las Vegas. He had some money and quite a few sheep. He talked three of us boys into taking some of his sheep on a share basis. We did this and gave him a mortgage on a part of our cattle. For a few years we did pretty well, then came a number of very dry years in succession. We lost so many sheep that we had to give R. some of our cattle. I lost so many sheep that it took all of my cattle to pay R. I lost everything I had. I paid him though, every penny of the debt, I paid him.

After this misfortune I began to work as a freighter. Used to travel between the towns of Las Vegas, Tucumcari, Santa Rosa, and Lincoln. I did this work for about 10 years. During this time I saved enough money to buy about 3 acres of the irrigated land in El Cerrito. There was no need to try to buy cattle or sheep again. The land around El Cerrito was taken up. I guess good times are gone from El Cerrito for good.

The social and political life of El Cerrito has changed during the history of the village much as has its broader base, the Southwest. Old timers in the village still talk of the yesterdays when life was much easier and people had time to think of something beside money and the means of getting it.

There was little emphasis put on schooling in the early days of settlement. No attempt was made to establish regular schools until after the American occupation of the territory in 1846.[5] All attempts at educating the children were initiated by the Church people and carried out by the priests or their helpers. As Blackmar has expressed it,

the Spanish colonist was not zealous in building up a new government, in developing the resources of the country, or in providing for the education of his children. As a rule, he himself was ignorant and knew little of the culture and refinement that result from educational advantages. Besides, had he desired it, there were no opportunities for education, either from books or from the world.[6]

---

[5]Lansing B. Bloom and Thomas C. Donnelly, *New Mexico History and Civics*, Albuquerque: The University Press, 1933, p. 193.

[6]Frank W. Blackmar, *op. cit., p.* 255.

The influence of the Church has always been great in the life of the people of El Cerrito and its sister settlements. The priest has ever been the best and almost only well informed person in the village and this alone has given him tremendous prestige among his simple followers. It has long been recognized that the local priest has been of extreme influence in all political elections. In 1939 an elderly priest in the area told the writer that he could swing the votes of his followers toward any political candidate he chose. There is little to doubt but that he was stating a fact. The influence of the Church in the small, rural villages of northern New Mexico is perhaps almost as strong today as it was fifty years ago.

Fifty years ago, the oldsters of El Cerrito will tell you, there were many forms of amusement in the village that no longer exist. Horse racing, *corridas de gallo*,[7] and many other types of games were frequently indulged in. There was an annual *fiesta* in the village in honor of the Patron Saint of the village. Friends and relatives came from miles around to join the villagers in their good times. Marriages, christenings, and any other affairs of comparable importance were celebrated in true holiday fashion. "Religious plays were presented during the Christmas season. Chants and hymns were an important part of church processions, of wakes, and of prayer meetings. Though the visit of some official, the birthday of a local leader, and similar events were often occasions for feasts and dances, the annual *fiestas* and other religious dates were the foundation

---

[7] A game, played on horses, in which a buried rooster is recovered.

of social life."[8] But the dances were the occasions when the peak of merriment was reached. To the tunes from a violin, guitar, and perhaps some other makeshift instrument, all able to walk without assistance swung around the dance floor at a pace that would make a neophyte dizzy. As a gay old man of the village described it to me, "the dances we used to have were something to remember. They would begin about 10 in the evening and last until sunup the next morning or until the wine got too strong for the legs that were carrying us. The dances they have now — they are nothing." I listened to his story patiently but after having attended several of the local dances and trying to maintain the furious pace they set until 3 o'clock in the morning, I had difficulty believing all of it.

THE LAND: OWNERSHIP AND USE

Land in El Cerrito, as in most Spanish-American villages in the area, falls into two major classes with modifications of each. They are:

1. Irrigable land
   a. Farm land
   b. Residential lots in the village
2. Dry or mesa land
   a. Cultivated
   b. Free grazing land

The irrigable land attached to the village of El Cerrito is limited in extent although each family either owns or is in line to inherit a small plot. Unfortunately, only a few have holdings sufficiently large to justify full-time farming or stock raising.

---

[8]George I. Sanchez, *Forgotten People, op. cit.,* p. 8.

This irrigable land is prized highly by the people of El Cerrito. Very little of it has ever been sold and then only to another resident of the village. This land is original grant land and has been handed down from parents to children for generations. Although the tracts are small (See Table II), this land is fertile and furnishes a considerable portion of the owner family's food.

TABLE II
SIZE OF HOLDINGS AND VALUE OF PROPERTY,
EL CERRITO, NEW MEXICO, 1940

	Number Reporting	Amount Reported (acres) Total	Average
Land Ownership:			
No Land Owned	1	0	0
Land owned	18*	2088.0	116.0
Dry land	14*	2070.5	172.54
Irrigated land	14	23.25	1.66
		Value of Property	
Land and buildings	18*	$6267.00	$348.00
Land only	18*	4622.00	231.00
House only	20	2445.00	122.00

*Excludes two owners who respectively own 1,292 and 2,000 acres of dry land.

For all 20 families who own dry land, the median owned is 42 acres.

The residential lots are also on original grant land and have been inherited. These lots were, for the most part, marked off at the time the village was settled. Any person born or otherwise coming into the village later, however, could still lay claim to a lot providing he could establish relationship with an original grantee or could gain the approval of the Board of Trustees set up to administer the grant land.

The dry or mesa land is much less valuable than the irrigable land and has never been greatly desired by the villagers. Only a few of the families have ever taken the trouble to increase their holdings by patenting or homesteading additional land.

As Table II shows, most of the families own some dry land. Some of this is usually farmed to beans or, if it is favorably located, to corn or wheat. As a rule, however, this land is not profitable for farming purposes because of the low rainfall in the area. Perhaps once in five years the dry land will produce a fairly satisfactory yield.

There is actually no free grazing land in the area but there are several sections of Public Domain near El Cerrito that may be grazed without protest. As might be imagined, this land is of the very poorest quality and any grazing benefits from it are negligible. Its chief value to the local people is as a source of firewood.

Several large tracts of land in the immediate vicinity of El Cerrito have come into the hands of non-resident owners, and other tracts have been donated to the Public School System of the state. This land is normally rented or leased to private stockmen for grazing purposes. The one large sheepman of El Cerrito has one school section and three sections of privately owned land leased for short terms. This land, however, is not available to the extent that it once was. Large sheep owners in the area have bought heavily of this grazing land with the result that little is now available for other than owner use.

The acute land shortage in the area began in 1916 when local townships were first surveyed and opened to homesteading. As this process went on, the boundaries of the land available to the people of El Cerrito gradually were drawn in. Some of this land was homesteaded by the villagers but most of the patents were

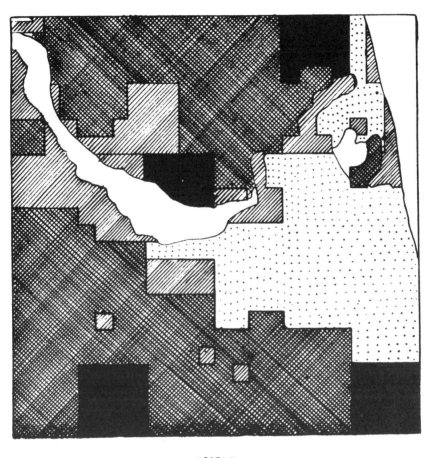

LEGEND
State Land   Federal Land (Open)
Owned by Outsiders   Locally Owned
Grant Land

Figure 4.   Ownership of Land for Township 12N, Range
15E, New Mexico.

sold almost as soon as they had been cleared for title. Figure 4 shows the manner in which the people of El Cerrito have been enclosed and the extent to which the land bordering on their irrigated tracts are owned by outsiders.

Actually the situation is much worse than Figure 4 indicates. Much of the dry land the villagers now own is of the poorest quality, often extremely rocky with no holes or streams of water. A few of the tracts are almost inaccessible because of steep hills, arroyos, or long stretches of fence that must be skirted.

TECHNIQUES OF AGRICULTURE

The agricultural techniques and practices in this area are archaic. Sons have truly followed in the footsteps of their fathers, and their sons, in turn, have followed after them. An early settler, returning to El Cerrito today, would find little change in crops grown or in the methods of cultivating and harvesting. Beans, corn, and alfalfa are planted year after year, with infrequent rotation. The one pronounced crop change has been the substitution of beans for wheat. Older residents claim that much more wheat was grown in the past when "rainfall was heavier and wheat flour difficult to buy." Only two local families are still growing wheat. All other families regard bean crops as more important. They are more likely to produce with scant rainfall and will add more to the family diet. It is more economical and desirable to be without flour than to be without beans.

The type of livestock kept is far below standard. Hogs, cows, and horses are of a scrubby, yet hardy breed, usually poor and carelessly tended. Few attempts have been made to improve the village's livestock. The villagers seem to prefer what they have and easily find rationalizations to justify their preference. Little information as to the advantages of better stock has been available to them, and any attempt to introduce such strange ideas would likely meet with some resistance. One of the local stockmen was persuaded to try improving his herd of cattle several years ago with little success.

Not only is the livestock owned in El Cerrito of a poor quality but it is extremely limited in numbers. See Table III. There are more horses and mules in the village than cows. The seven cows owned are inadequate to supply more than a small fraction of the dairy products the people would need for a satisfactory diet. In fact, very little milk is drunk even by the small children. Instead, it is to a large extent passed around to the neighbors for use in coffee and, to a limited extent, in cooking. In brief, aside from the two large owners in the village, livestock has come to play only a minor role in the economy of these people.

TABLE III
NUMBER OF SPECIFIED LIVESTOCK OWNED BY FAMILIES
OF EL CERRITO, NEW MEXICO, 1940

Type of Livestock	Number Reporting Livestock	Number Reported	
		Total	Average per Family
Horses and mules	17	36	2.1
Cows	7*	23	3.3
Chickens	8	82	10.3
Sheep	2	—**	——
Goats	1	81*	——
Hogs	1	1	1

*Excludes 2 owners of large acreages who respectively reported 25 and 30 cows. One of these also reported 500 head of sheep and 81 goats.
**Besides one large owner only one family had sheep — 2 head.

The same things could be said of their poultry. It is as mixed as it likely could be. Seemingly, the people neither keep them for meat or the eggs they will lay. One of the elderly women of the village informed me that she never ate one of her chickens and that they very seldom layed an egg. To the question of "why do you keep them?" she answered, quite simply, "We keep them for household pets."

It is probable that better livestock would not receive proper care and treatment. Shelters are not available, even during the severe parts of the winter months. No one would think of calling a veterinary if a cow or horse should become sick or injured. Native stock is treated with home remedies that require only the simplest of ingredients such as lard, salt, or native herbs.

The farm equipment and machinery used in this area is of the simplest kind. Large machinery is neither used nor appreciated. A horse, a ten-inch turning plow, and a few hoes and a pitchfork make up the standard equipment of a farm. The plow is used to turn the soil, plant the crop, and cultivate it. Wheat and beans are threshed by hand with the flail. If the crop is large enough to justify it, horses or goats may aid in the threshing by walking back and forth on the grain until it becomes separated and settles to the bottom of the pile. The grain is cleaned by means of winnowing. Women and children help in this farm task.

Alfalfa is the sole crop that is not harvested by hand tools. Two of the families have horse-drawn mowing machines which cut most of the alfalfa in the valley as custom work. The owners of the machines are given a portion of the alfalfa or its equivalent in labor as payment for cutting it. Cash is never involved in the exchange.

Plowing and planting operations begin in late May or the early part of June. The date may vary from two to three weeks, depending upon the mildness of the season or the quantity of moisture in the soil. The two operations are usually carried out simultaneously. As the soil is being turned, the seeds are dropped into each third furrow.

The village has only one planter. It is a walking planter, pulled by one horse and capable of planting one row at a time. The owner is regarded as the most modern farmer in the village although he received some criticism for his investments in more efficient tools. The people feel that time and labor are of minor value. Efficiency and time saving mean little where already man power is far in excess of the work to be done.

Intensive cultivation of crops begins in the latter part of June. Beans and corn are plowed from three to five times, depending upon the rainfall and the number of times the land is irrigated. The crops are weeded and thinned when, according to local standards, these operations are necessary. These tasks fall to the boys, aided at intervals by the father. Alfalfa, which besides harvesting requires about three irrigations in spring and summer, entails less labor than any other crop grown on the irrigable land. It is usually re-seeded only once in each five to seven years.

The irrigation system in use by the many villages along the Pecos river in New Mexico is an old one.

No one in El Cerrito remembers when it was built. However, there is considerable evidence that it was built originally by the Indians. The present course of the ditch has been unchanged for many years. Evidence of this is found in the many feet of bank that have been built up by annual cleanings. Even in places where construction of the ditch would have necessitated removal of only a few feet of dirt, the height of the lower bank has risen to ten feet or more. The *madre acequia,* or main ditch, is slightly less than two miles long. It begins at a bottle-neck part of the river where a crude dam has been built. This dam was constructed by laying a line of stone across the river and stacking brush and long poles behind it. In this way the bed of the river, above the dam, has been raised a height of approximately six feet. This added elevation enables the water to flow out into the main ditch and on to the valley land below.

The construction of the dam is such that there is little assurance of its permanence. Any big flood or unusual flow of water may destroy the entire structure.[9] No provision is made for diversion, hence the dam must carry the weight and pressure of any quantity of water that happens to come against it. If the pressure is too great, the dam is destroyed, as are the crops below which are dependent upon it. Before it can be restored lack of water has possibly killed the crops in the valley.

From the dam the main ditch runs along the river,

---

[9]In 1935 a heavy rain in the Upper Pecos Watershed destroyed the local dam completely. Before it could be replaced crops were burned out resulting in a total crop loss for the year.

but the fall in the ditch is less than in the river, so that at the entrance to the valley it carries its water many feet above the surface of the river. This main ditch, and its smaller tributaries, are maintained and repaired communally by the users of the water. The organization for carrying out these tasks is one of the most highly integrated and efficient in the community. Its chief functions are carried on by a *mayordomo,* or ditch boss, who supervises all work on the system, and a committee which is responsible for all rules governing the use of the water. Each user must contribute labor on the ditch in proportion to the amount of irrigated land he operates. The officers are elected annually by the people. There is seldom an occasion for interference or supervision of the use of the water. Water is plentiful, so it is available for anyone needing it with never a wait longer than two or three days.

There are no intense and extended seasons of farm labor in El Cerrito. Although such tasks as planting, cultivating, and harvesting require a few days of intense effort, they are soon over and the farmer is again able to distribute his time and labor over a wide variety of tasks. A full day's labor during the busiest season is spiced with periods of relaxation. Although the worker may rise early and go about feeding and caring for his domestic livestock, there is no hurry at breakfast time. After breakfast and a brief planning of the day's work, he is off for the field until 11 or 11:30. The noon meal consumes a good half hour, followed by one or two hours of *siesta.* The afternoon's work in the field assumes the same tempo. The farmer is usually back home when the sun is still high for supper and to do the evening chores around the house. He attends to the horses and the cow, if there is one, after the evening meal is over. Throughout the day he has had time for brief chats and frequent exchanges of advice with passing friends or relatives. In brief, there is little rushing brought about by time or season. Caring for the average local farm unit necessitates little haste. One is able to choose here between a slow tempo and a more complete use of time. The native usually favors the former.

HEALTH AND MEDICAL FACILITIES

Several recent studies in the vicinity of El Cerrito emphasize the poor health and sanitary conditions of the people.[10] Water for family use is taken from the river or irrigation ditch to which all livestock have access. In many cases the sanitary facilities are located in such a manner that their drainage flows into the river. As a result epidemics may sweep the entire village, as well as others in the vicinity, within a very short time. An attempt has been made in recent years to get the people to boil their drinking water but with little success. Most of them will say that "the water doesn't taste good after it has been boiled."

A doctor is seldom called to attend a sick person in El Cerrito. The distance is too great and the cost is prohibitive. The native superstitions of the people would occasion much distrust of a doctor's modern means of treating sickness. Instead, they rely on home remedies and patent medicine.[11]

---

[10]See Sanchez, *op. cit.*, pp. 66-67; San Miguel Rural Council, *A Survey of Villanueva*, Las Vegas: Highlands University, 1936, p. 24; Glenn Grisham, *El Pueblo*, unpublished survey of the village of El Pueblo, New Mexico.
[11]See Appendix for partial list of home remedies used in El Cerrito.

All maternity cases in the village are attended by midwives. There is no midwife in El Cerrito but there are two in the nearest village to El Cerrito. These midwives are highly regarded by the local people and can be called in for a nominal charge. A few of the younger men of the village expressed a preference for a trained doctor's services but added that they could not afford the regular doctor's fee.

Many of the infants born in El Cerrito die within a few weeks or months of their birth. It is nothing unusual to learn that a comparatively young married couple has lost one or more of their children at an early age. A large per cent of these deaths occur under six months of age. As Table IV shows, once a child born in El Cerrito has attained the age of one year he has a good chance of living. Sixteen of the children reported as having died under five years of age were under six months of age. It is very likely that all of these deaths were not reported. Several of the older families had difficulty in remembering whether one, two, or three of their children had died.

TABLE IV
NUMBER OF CHILDREN WHO WERE REPORTED AS
HAVING DIED UNDER 5 YEARS OF AGE,
EL CERRITO, NEW MEXICO, 1940

Age at Death	Number of Children
Total	36
Under 6 months	16
6 months - 1 year	13
1 year - 2 years	3
2 years - 3 years	2
3 years - 4 years	2
4 years - 5 years	—

RECREATION AND AMUSEMENT

As in the past, indicated above, there are few forms of amusement or recreation in El Cerrito that are not associated with the Church. No games are played by the adults in the village, and the games played by the children are simple and usually "homespun." A few of the older men spend a few days each summer fishing although, this activity is practiced more for meat than for sport.

The one form of recreation generally indulged in and enjoyed by everyone, old and young alike, is the dances or the *bailes*. These dances are held almost every Saturday night and often during the week when the people are less busy with their crops or outside work.

These dances are attended almost exclusively by local folk, and the music is always home talent. The musical instruments are: a violin, a guitar, and infrequently an accordion. The music is largely old Spanish tunes such as the *raspa*, the *varcoviano*, and others of similar rhythm and tempo. During recent years there has been some influx of modern Anglo tunes but the native people, as a rule, do not appreciate them.

There is little variation in the manner in which these dances are conducted. There is an accepted procedure in initiating them which is never deviated from in the slightest. Thus, as is true of so many other phases of the people's lives, the dances long ago assumed a pattern that has become accepted and about which there is, seemingly, no desire for change.

The first step in promoting a local dance is the selection of a sponsor. Such a person may be requested to sponsor the dance or may do it on his own initiative. He is usually an unmarried boy with enough money to pay the small costs. Such costs include a fee (25 cents) to the local Justice of the Peace for granting a permit and enough gasoline to keep three gasoline lamps burning through the greater part of the night. In case the sponsor does not have an ample stock of his own vintage the costs may also include a bottle of wine for each of the musicians.

The dances are seldom announced before sundown of the day on which they are to be given. At that time the musicians make a round of the *plaza,* playing their instruments and followed by the small boys and most of the many dogs of the village. The noise made by the musicians is greatly augmented by the shouts of the boys and the barking of the dogs.

These dances are always held in the schoolhouse. Chairs, desks and other school equipment are cleared away with the exception of a single row of seats that run along each side of the building. These seats are so placed for the benefit of the aged and the younger dancers during the several brief rest periods of the evening.

The crowd begins to gather about 10 o'clock, filing in small groups. The girls must come in groups or in company with their parents as no unmarried daughter would be allowed to come alone or in company with an unrelated male. They file slowly into the building, the girls seating themselves on one side of the room and the boys on the opposite side. This division of the sexes is maintained throughout the evening except when the dances are in progress.

As mentioned above, the dance tunes are largely of Spanish or Mexican origin and generally are of an extremely fast tempo. The dancing couples swing around at an amazing rate of speed which one can hardly believe possible to maintain for more than a brief period of time. As a rule the male does the greater part of the dancing while his partner assumes a more stoical role of following him around.

The old people, as well as the young, attend these dances regularly. It is seldom that a person stays away that is physically able to attend. Many of the older people dance and, despite their age, seem to have almost as much stamina as the younger people. Those who are too old to dance usually stay until the dance is over; which may be from two until four o'clock in the morning. Children are brought along and by midnight are stretched out on benches, in corners, and in the laps of their mothers all around the room.

Although these dances are enjoyed tremendously by everyone, young and old, they are, primarily, a form of recreation for the young. They are almost the only recognized means of contact between the unmarried boys and girls. As a result, most of the dances are sponsored and paid for by the young, unmarried males of the village.

RELIGION AND THE CHURCH

The people of El Cerrito are 100 per cent Catholic. The Church and its teachings play a tremendously important role in the attitudes, practices, and everyday life of these people. It is the earnest desire of every individual to live entirely within the doctrine of the church.

El Cerrito has no resident priest. The village is too

small and poor to support one. The priest that serves El Cerrito lives in the nearby village of Villanueva. He comes to the village once a month to conduct mass and to hear confessions. In case of a death, or a similar emergency, he may make a special visit, but the average year would necessitate no more than two or three extra visits. Absence of the priest, however, does not mean that religious services are not held regularly at least once per week. The people congregate each Sunday and sometimes as frequently as every day of the week in the church. These extra services are in charge of a local woman who is selected and paid a small fee by the Church.

The services are conducted in a very humble spirit. The women seat themselves on the benches and the men kneel on the hard floor in the rear of the church. The attendance is usually good. There are never many who are able to rationalize staying away. All present take part in the services. The hymns and ritual that are part of the service are well learned, even by the very small children.

After the services are over the men meet in front of the church for a half-hour or more of conversation. This is as much a part of the service as any of the formalized ritual. Such meetings afford the men their most frequent opportunity for getting together in a group. The conversation is directed to the entire group. The topics are generally local happenings or any news a recent visitor has brought back from town. The group never breaks up until each man who has something to offer has had his say.

The local priest serving El Cerrito has a status not

approached by any other individual in the locality. This is easily understood when it is realized that he is the sole and undisputed representative of the Church and the only man in the area with any significant amount of formal education. Consequently, his word is authority and seldom questioned on worldly or on religious matters. During the recent period of heavy relief in the area (1933-1940) many priests assumed the responsibility of acting as intermediary between the people and the governmental agencies operating in that part of the state. The policies and procedures of these agencies were new to the people and the priest was the only source for clearance. Many local agency representatives are frank to admit that securing the support of the priest often meant the difference between the success or failure of a program in a particular village.

The Church in El Cerrito is not self-supporting. Although meager monthly contributions are made by the people, these are not sufficient to absorb the total cost of the Church's program. When asked about their annual church dues none of the families estimated they gave more than $5 per year.

In addition to regular services the Church sponsors other activities in the village. In one of these the village holds each year a community function in honor of its Patron Saint. This celebration is one of the most gala affairs of the year. This function is held in December and lasts for two full days. Elaborate rules and procedures have evolved to govern the affair. Although the villagers sponsor and conduct the function, the priest is always invited to attend as the guest of honor.

Two leaders are elected each year to be responsible for the conduct of the function. It is their duty to invite the priest, to provide food and drink for all, to open their homes to accommodate the guests, and to supervise any other details of the affair. It is considered an honor to hold one of these posts, and, providing he can finance the several costs, a man regards himself as fortunate to be elected. The financial status of the candidates is always taken into consideration in the election in order that the candidates elected may be able to assume the financial responsibility. The term of office is for one year only. No one man is expected to serve two years in succession although the same man often serves in alternate years.

These functions begin on the eve of the Patron Saint's birthday. Food and drink have been made ready in large quantities and spread out in the houses of the two church leaders who were elected at the function the previous year. Visitors, neighbors, and relatives file in and out of the houses at will, partaking of the feast at their pleasure. This continues until late in the afternoon, when everyone marches to the church for special service. After the service is over they come back to the houses, where they may again take food and drink if they so desire. The last feature of the evening is the dance which, like the others, begins at about 10 o'clock in the evening and lasts until early morning. The second day of the affair is simply a duplicate of the first.

Another feature, celebrated in El Cerrito and highly typical of the area, is the strict observance of Holy Friday. This is an event which prohibits all sorts of manual labor for the day before, the day after, and including Holy Friday. It is the one time of the year when all the villagers wear their best clothes and the men are clean shaven.

Church services are held during the morning, afternoon and again in the evening on Holy Friday. Each of these services is announced by the clatter of an old wooden *matraca* that looks very much like an ancient coffee grinder. The church bell is silent until the final services are over.

The observance of Holy Friday by the people of El Cerrito is not a somber occasion. On the whole it is a gay affair, a time for neighboring and friendly exchange of gossip. It is a day when the homemakers vie with one another in the preparation and exchange of food. Small boys and girls are kept continuously busy running from one house to the next with trays of food to be sampled.

SOCIAL PARTICIPATION

As table V clearly indicates, the formal social life of the El Cerrito people is extremely limited if participation in church services is excluded. Out of a total of 183 formal meetings of all organizations held during the year 154 were church service meetings. The attendance at these meetings was approximately the same for the male and female family heads.

Next to the church services, dances were the most frequently attended of all social events. Of the 26 formal dances held during the year 1939, each male and female head reported having attended 50 per cent of the time. Personal observation over a major portion of the year 1940 leads the writer to believe that the actual attendance figure, for both male and female heads, was considerably higher.

TABLE V
SOCIAL PARTICIPATION OF HEADS OF FAMILIES,
EL CERRITO, NEW MEXICO, 1939

Type of Gathering	Number of Meetings in year	Average Number of Times Attended		Average Expend- iture per Family	Average Distance to Meeting Place
		Male	Female		
Religious meetings	154	144.4	146.1	$3.21	81.7 yds.
Educational meetings	1	1	0	0	79.4 yds.
Ditch commission	1	1	0	0	82.4 yds.
Political meetings	1	1	0	0	83.3 yds.
Dances	26	13.4	13.4	0	

The money cost of participation in the local social life was almost nil as may be seen from Table V. None of the families indicated any expense for these items outside the church. The average figure for church expenditure was only $3.21 per family.

Although these figures indicate a very meager formal social life for these people adequate figures would show an abundance of informal social participation. The physical structure of this village greatly facilitates informal contacts. All houses in the village are within a stone's thrown of one another. See Figure 1. Through years of interdependence, the people are conditioned to call upon neighbors and relatives for many types of assistance and, in turn, are expected to reciprocate when the need arises. Any task that requires greater strength or physical effort than a single family has at hand is solved by calling in one or more neighbors. Such service is freely asked for and given. In case of sickness or similar misfortune the efforts and resources of the entire village may be utilized in order to bring the family through the crisis.

Informal visiting far exceeds any other mode of contact between the villagers. The latchstring is "always on the outside" for any neighbor or relative who may have the time and inclination to call. In a single afternoon fourteen different visitors were counted coming to one household, some of them returning as many as three and four times. This was not a peculiar case. Other homes in the village probably had as many. Such visits are expected. If a housewife fails to make a call in the afternoon it is taken for granted that she is ill or else has company.

Although visiting is general in El Cerrito, the degree of blood relationship is the chief factor affecting their frequency. The house of the parents of several married sons and daughters is the nucleus for the different visiting groups. The wives and children of such families may come to the central house a dozen or more times in a day. They come to distribute a bit of news or to borrow a little something for the next meal. The children are running into and out of each other's houses so much it is difficult for an outsider to learn the houses in which they belong.

Although the visiting of the women far exceeds that of the men, each day affords the men ample opportunities for contacts and conversation. After a day in the field is over they are likely to meet for a short time around the house or in going or coming from the corrals. Also for the men there are other opportunities for contacts, such as the field work, the local meetings, and the trips to town.

Little visiting is done outside the village. This is especially true of the women, who seldom see a woman from the outside. The majority of the women of El Cerrito do not leave their village more than once or twice each year.

Family visits outside the village are usually to the homes of relatives in the larger towns. Such trips serve three main purposes: a chance to remain in town for a few days, a chance to make periodic purchases, and a chance to visit with friends and relatives as long as a week. These visits are seldom repaid. Such hospitality is accepted by both parties as an obligation the town people owe their country relatives.

MARRIAGE AND THE FAMILY

There are only a few adults in El Cerrito who have never married. For a boy or girl to remain unmarried too long is to risk a loss of status in the village. This is especially true for the girls for whom there is no other career than to become a housewife and mother.

The vast majority of the people marry at a relatively early age. See Table VI. Of the 19 unbroken families living in the village, eleven of the female heads had been married under twenty years of age and eleven of the male heads had been married under 24 years of age. Only two women married the first time after they were 25 years old. The average age at marriage for both male and female heads was less than 22 years.[12]

-----

[12] A tabulation of the records of the local church revealed that, out of 296 marriages contracted within the local area and during the last 25 years, all but a small fraction of both males and females were married under 25 years of age. When plotted on a graph two modal ages were revealed for the men, the first at 21 and the second at 36.

TABLE VI

AGE AT MARRIAGE OF MALE AND FEMALE HEADS OF
HOUSEHOLDS, EL CERRITO, NEW MEXICO, 1940

Age at Marriage	Total	Male	Female
Average age	21.7	24	19
Under 20 years	11	0	11
20 - 24 years	17	11	6
25 - 29 years	9	7	2
30 - 34 years	1	1	0
Total	38	19	19

Marriage is an event in the life of an El Cerrito boy or girl that is equalled in importance by few other occasions. The ceremony, and the process leading up to it, are equally ritualistic in the formal manner in which they are practiced. The exotic features of both are Spanish, or perhaps Roman, in origin and have become only slightly modified in a hundred years of contact with another culture.

Until approximately twenty years ago local marriages were influenced greatly by the parents. In this manner land and other property holdings could be consolidated advantageously. Recently, however, this practice has become much less common and a boy or girl may choose his own mate with little interference from parents or other relatives.

The parents still play a minor role in the matchmaking even though it is only a vestige of the authority they once wielded. The prospective bridegroom's parents, usually the mother, still visits the parents of the bride-to-be and discusses the match with them. After the discussion she leaves a pumpkin with them and if the pumpkin is not returned the match is considered made.

The bridegroom furnishes the trousseau of the bride. Since this is somewhat expensive and since, too, he must have "open-house" on the day of the wedding, it is sometimes extremely difficult for the boy to accumulate enough wealth to finance a wedding. A number of the younger men of the village admitted to the writer that their weddings were postponed for from one to five years as a result of their inability to accumulate sufficient funds for the ceremony.

The day of the wedding a spirit of *fiesta* pervades the village. The parents of the groom have given their house over to the young couple and enough food and wine for all has been prepared. The doors of the house are kept open all day and the villagers may come in for food or drink at any time they choose.

The wedding usually takes place in the morning, either in the local village or in the village in which the priest lives. After the ceremony the couple must go to the *plaza* to have their picture taken in their new finery. This is almost as important as any part of the ceremony. Such pictures are distributed to many close relatives and one is always brought back to be hung in the house. This is about the only occasion in the life of either bride or groom when there is opportunity or the clothes to really "dress up."

After the ceremony has been performed and the pictures taken the bride and groom return to the village where they are the hosts to the villagers. This continues until the evening when all attend a dance which has also been sponsored and paid for by the groom. These dances may well last until 4 or 5 o'clock in the morning as everyone tries, as long as possible, to keep the new couple from going home.

The entire set of values by which the local people

live are woven around the institutions of family and
Church. Loyalties, responsibilities, and duties are primarily connected with the meaning of family. The es-
teem for an individual in the community comes out
of contributions or failure in relation to this institution. The primary virtues that give an individual or
a family prestige in the village spring from the conduct
of the family group. Family in El Cerrito means more
than parents and offspring. It also, in the real sense,
includes grandparents and grandchildren as well.

In the El Cerrito family the father is definitely the
head. His word is family law and, within all bounds of
reason, will be recognized as such by the other people
of the village. It is the father who makes all final decisions, handles the finances, and provides for the welfare of the family. The place of the mother is in the
home. It is her duty to look after the household, do
the household chores, and bear and rear children.

To be recognized as a good citizen of El Cerrito a
man must support, not only his own immediate family,
but give what aid he can to parents or to any other
relatives in need. Failure to do this brings social cen-
sure in its most formidable form. Living in accordance
with this code brings respect of the highest order.

There is a very high degree of blood relationship
between the families of El Cerrito. This is well demon-
strated by the fact that there are only seven family
names in the village. Each family is at least distantly
related to every other family. In fact, these blood relationships have increased over the years to the extent
that no marriages have taken place between the local
villagers within the past fifteen years. The last mar-

riage was severely censured by the local priest because the bride and groom were second cousins.

EDUCATION

The school building in El Cerrito is an antiquated, two-room structure that was evidently built with little more than a certain amount of space in mind. The furnishings and equipment are in keeping with the building. The lighting arrangement is very poor and the heating system consists of two wood-burning stoves, one for each room.

This crude building houses from twenty to fifty pupils, depending upon attendance, in addition to the two teachers. Instruction is given in grades one to eight inclusive. The school is conducted with little supervision from the county system. Roads are too poor and the distance from the county seat too great for a supervisor to come to El Cerrito more than once or twice during a school year.

Attendance at the school is poor. The girls attend more regularly than the boys, especially after reaching the higher grades. After a boy has reached the age of twelve or thirteen he is expected to aid in supporting the family and is often kept out of school to help the father or to hire out to anyone needing his services. For this reason, few of the boys complete the full eight grades of schooling offered unless they do so at a very early age. See Table VII.

As table VII indicates, the girls usually continue in school longer than do the boys. Eighteen of the females reported having completed eight years of schooling or more as compared with sixteen of the males.

TABLE VII

GRADES IN SCHOOL COMPLETED BY MALES AND FEMALES
ABOVE 15 YEARS OF AGE AND NOT ATTENDING SCHOOL
EL CERRITO, NEW MEXICO, 1940*

Grades Completed	Total	Male	Female
Total	94	45	49
Under 2 grades	1	1	0
2 - 3 grades	17	7	10
4 - 5 grades	16	9	7
6 - 7 grades	26	12	14
8 - 9 grades	24	9	15
10 grades and over	10	7	3

*These figures include family members now living elsewhere.

The males, however, more frequently went beyond eight grades. This, obviously, indicates schooling away from the village which would not be permissible for the girls unless they could live, while away from home, with a near relative.

The program of the El Cerrito school involves no other persons than the teachers and enrolled children. Parents are neither consulted nor do they volunteer any advice relative to the school and its program. The general concensus seems to be that the teachers are hired and paid to conduct the school and can do it best without any interference from the outside.

There are two occasions during the year when parents are invited to visit the school. One is at the end of the school term and the other on Christmas Eve. At each of these occasions, the children produce a short play on which they have been practicing for several months. In these productions the children are given an opportunity to demonstrate to their elders, their ability to speak English. Although the words are quite often unintelligible the parents are usually highly pleased at the progress their progeny have made. If the parents are pleased the teachers know they have had a successful year.

Despite its many limitations the local people regard this school as one of the most important institutions of the village. It is generally regarded as serving the purpose of orientating the children to the outside world and to some extent to be bridging the gap that separates the two. Although few parents expect their children to complete more than eight grades of school, this minimum is considered to be highly valuable. Any less, they believe, does not give one an adequate mastery of English.

Few local opinions are ever heard expressed as to how or what the schools should teach. Other than English and arithmetic there is little consideration given by the parents to what their children are being taught. It is generally believed, however, that the primary function of the schools is to teach English. If the schools do a satisfactory job of teaching arithmetic and English the people are satisfied. The remainder of what a child should know can be taught by the Church and in the home.

Despite the desire of the parents to have their children learn English well, it is seldom that a local boy or girl attains any degree of proficiency in the use of this language. The girls usually speak it much better than the boys, probably as a result of their longer and more regular attendance at school.

From a standpoint of educational achievement the teaching personnel of the local school is usually of the poorest quality. It is difficult to induce well trained teachers to come into isolated villages such as El Cerrito where living conditions are so difficult and salaries so low. During the year of survey both teachers were of local extraction, one of them from the village. Since these teachers knew Spanish it was extremely difficult to force the students to speak English although a state statute requires that nothing but English be spoken on the school grounds.

Teaching techniques and materials are not adapted to the peculiar problems met in the local school situation.[13] The sole means for imparting knowledge is a group of standardized textbooks. Any other equipment is devised by the teachers and fashioned out of tin cans, boxes and other crude materials at hand. No consideration is given to the fact that the pupils are learning a new language in addition to stock materials which they are required to master. Such subject matter as geography, history, and health is taught in terms entirely foreign to the pupils' experience and background. During the school year 1939-40 a visit to one of the classrooms disclosed that the pupils were being required to work out posters and other manual projects based on such phenomena as transportation in Boston and the importance of geography in the growth of Chicago. Under such a curriculum as this it is small wonder that pupil interest is at a minimum and that progress is slow.

POLITICS

Politics, as a form of activity, is participated in by all the male adults of El Cerrito. Election "season" is looked forward to with a great deal of enthusiasm, al-

---

[13]Sanchez, op. cit., pp. 71-88.

though there have been few candidates for county office, from the village, in the history of its settlement.

The area in which El Cerrito is located has long been regarded by county politicians as the area in which a county election may easily be decided. A local story has it that, until comparatively recently, a candidate favorable to the area used to call the big sheep men of the area the afternoon of the election and ask "how many votes do you have for me?" The answer would be "how many do you need?" and the necessary ballots would be hurried into the county seat. This gave rise to a still current expression of "voting the sheep."

Until 1932 the village was 100 per cent Republican. At that time it voted a unanimous Democratic ticket and it has remained Democratic in all subsequent elections. In a recent state election the villagers voted solidly against a Republican candidate for a state office even though the candidate was a native Spanish-American product.

A candidate for any office is appraised in El Cerrito in terms of "what can he do for us." Political, moral, or religious principles are of scondary importance. His attitude toward national or state issues that do not concern them directly is given scant attenion. Instead, he is measured in terms of the number of jobs and the amount of grants and relief he has obtained or is likely to obtain for his constituents. In El Cerrito, these are the things that matter.

Much of the machinery for operating local politics is old. Office holders and new candidates still court and retain the good will of their constituents by means of free dances, free drinks, and now and then a *fiesta*.[14] These "hand-outs" are expected and a candidate that would choose not to cater to the voters in this manner would have little chance of winning an election. People are induced to come into town by the score when one of these events is announced.

To the old political machinery in the area there have been added recently, certain small, new clubs, through which the people are able more directly to make their needs and voting strength known. Predominant in this field have been the political clubs which cater to the younger people. These clubs are operating in most of the little villages of the area, El Cerrito not excepted. These clubs have their own elected officers. Infrequent meetings are held in which the men discuss their political problems in their own way.

Any political meeting or rally in El Cerrito incites a great deal of enthusiasm and draws a good attendance. The village has its well-recognized best speakers who are always present to talk at great length and in glowing terms of their favorite candidates. Such meetings are dynamic affairs, thoroughly enjoyed by all present. The political issue or candidate is often completely lost sight of in the light of a passionate and dramatic address. Such speeches are remembered and discussed more from the standpoint of presentation by the speaker than from any content the speech might have had.

The village of El Cerrito is peculiar in this area in

14These practices have encouraged a great deal of graft in the local government. A candidate for county office in 1940 told the author that the office, which paid little more than $100 per month, would net him $10,000 in two years in office.

that it has no acute internal political difficulties. The fact that the village has no factions enables the people to work in unison. This could be duplicated in only a few Spanish-American villages in San Miguel county. In most of the villages two or more antagonistic factions exist that preclude any possibility of the people working together as a group.

LEVEL OF LIVING

In terms of cash income and material goods the families of El Cerrito are certainly not above the poverty line.[15] The average cash family income for the calendar year of 1939 was only $294.[16] See Table VIII. This was $50 per family less than a village studied in the lower Rio Grande area of New Mexico in 1938.[17]

TABLE VIII
AVERAGES FOR SPECIFIED ITEMS, EL CERRITO,
NEW MEXICO, 1940

Item	Number Reporting	Average Reported
Age of dwelling, years	20	63.7
Size of dwelling, rooms	20	3.35
Size of household, number	21	6.33
Distance to water supply, yards	21	96.19
Family, off farm income, dollars (wages) .	18*	294.0

* Excludes 2 owners of large acreages and one teacher. No cash income from farm for any but 3 families.

As pointed out earlier, the little patches of irrigated

---

[15]B. S. Rowntree, *Poverty, A Study of Town Life*, New York: Longmans, Green and Co., 1922, p. 160.

[16]Although this figure does not include products sold from the farm such items were negligible in 1939. Only 3 families sold products from their farms in 1939 all of which aggregated less than $100, with the exception of sheep and cattle sold by two of the three families.

[17]C. P. Loomis and O. E. Leonard, *Standards of Living in an Indian-Mexican Village and on a Reclamation Project*, Washington: United States Department of Agriculture, B. A. E., Social Research Report No. XIV, 1938, p. 13.

land in the village make living in the local valley possible with the aid of the little cash earned from working outside. Such patches are usually sufficient in extent to produce almost all the food that goes on the table during the growing season and provide some food, in the way of canned fruits and vegetables, for the winter months.

Although the houses are small and old (see Table VIII) they are fairly adequate for the climate. Constructed of adobe, a sun dried brick of mud and straw, they provide excellent protection from the cold winters and ample insulation against the heat of the summer months.

Such houses can be constructed at an amazingly low cash cost. No materials need be bought outside of windows and doors unless the family is financially able to purchase sheet iron roofing and wooden flooring. At the time of the writer's stay in the village in 1940 a newly married man built a three-room house for a total cash outlay of $87 which included the rough board flooring. Had he chosen to endure dirt floors the cost would have been considerably less.

The furniture in these houses is generally scant and of the simplest construction. Some of it is handmade but this is a craft that is rapidly disappearing in the area. A typical bedroom will contain no more than a bed or two, a table, stove, and possibly a chest of drawers. The kitchen furniture will consist of a stove, table and either some benches or chairs.

The drinking and other water for the household is carried in pails from the irrigation ditch which runs along the village boundary. This water is carried by the women and small children over an average distance of approximately 100 yards.

Clothing costs are held at a minimum. Very little new clothing is bought except at special occasions such as a wedding, or the annual confirmation of the children by the Church. Clothing is handed down extensively from larger to smaller brother or sister. More fortunate relatives are depended upon heavily for gifts of cast-off shoes, suits, dresses, and hats.

V

THE ROLE OF THE LAND GRANT IN THE SOCIAL ORGANIZATION AND SOCIAL PROCESSES OF A SPANISH-AMERICAN VILLAGE IN NEW MEXICO

ALMOST 350 years ago the first contingent of Spanish-speaking colonists arrived in the territory of New Mexico to begin a period of settlement in the area that has continued to the present time. The early Spanish colonists brought with them, as part of their cultural heritage, a definite scheme for settling the land. This scheme included such factors as: a definite form or pattern of settlement, specific ways and measures for dividing the land among themselves, and pre-conceived ideas of land tenure and other social relationships between the population and the land.

Settlements in New Mexico were almost universally located on existing streams of water in order that the families could carry on the combination enterprises of irrigated agriculture and stock-raising. This practice was continued throughout the Spanish and Mexican period of occupation and still remains as a striking feature of the cultural landscape.

Dry or pasture lands were abundantly available, stretching out in every direction from the settlement center. Private titles were granted to some of this land

and that remaining was used with no thought of exclusion or trespass. Irrigated holdings, on the other hand, were limited and assigned to individuals. In dividing this irrigated land the river or other stream frontage was the place of departure. Usually the holdings consisted of long, narrow strips that might extend across the entire village settlement.

Titles to the land were granted by the Spanish Crown and later by the Mexican Republic. They were usually phrased in ambiguous and indefinite terms in respect to both the territory granted and the rights extended. Boundary lines were vague and confusing, stretching from one natural object to another and utilizing many markers that might change or else disappear altogether over a short period.

Until the American occupation of the territory in 1846, the problems of indefinite and indeterminate boundaries, legal titles of ownership, and indiscriminate use of the land were not particularly acute. Density of population was slight at this time and ample grazing land for all seems to have been available.

When the area became a part of the United States, however, the task of establishing definite boundaries and titles began, a process that lasted until early in the 1900's. This task was extremely complicated by a number of factors such as lack of adequate records, reticence on the part of the people to submit claims, and perhaps most fundamental, the many difficulties involved in the superimposing of one type of land system upon another. [1]

---

[1]The United States has adopted the rectangular system of land division and the Spanish and Mexican governments used the river front and indefinite natural boundaries.

It is the proposition of this study that these physical factors, in their early nature and in subsequent changes, have been of some considerable influence on the social organization, institutions, and social processes of the people in contact with them. As Smith has pointed out such social factors as "the relationships of farmers' dwellings to the land and to one another is basic to all rural social organization and consequently a logical beginning for any analysis of the structure of rural society."[2] The nature of this influence as revealed by the study of a selected Spanish-American village, and something of its extent, is developed in the following pages.

BRIEF HISTORY OF THE LAND GRANT IN NEW MEXICO

The land problem in New Mexico has probably been as tangled as it has in any of the other states of the Union. Land grants from the Crown of Spain, succeeded by those given by the Mexican Republic, and finally the inclusion of a large part of New Mexico in the Public Domain of the United States, all combined to produce a state of confusion that took a half-century of litigation, plus survey after survey, to untangle. Not only have the people of New Mexico been immeshed in numerous disputes and legal complications, but the contests over titles have involved people of other states and other countries as well. As a student of the public land policy of the United States has ob-

---

[2] T. Lynn Smith, "An Analysis of Rural Social Organization Among the French-speaking people of Southern Louisiana," *Journal of Farm Economics*, XVI, 1939, p. 680.

served without exaggeration relative to a large New Mexico grant of land, "it affected high officials or prominent business men in America, England and Holland. It produced guerilla warfare in New Mexico and wild scrambles on the Amsterdam stock exchange."[3]

The oldest grant in the state of New Mexico, of which there is record, is the Cieneguilla grant located in Santa Fe County. The petition for this grant was allowed by the Spanish Crown in 1693 and confirmed by the United States government in 1899. There are doubtless many older grants in the state, the papers for which have long been lost or destroyed.[4]

There are no records available which indicate the exact number of land grants conferred by the Spanish Crown in New Mexico, nor even approximate figures as to the acreages included in them.[5]

That the number must have been a hundred or more, however, is indicated by the fact that between the years 1693 and 1821 a total of 61 were granted and retained sufficient evidence of title as to be confirmed by the United States government after its possession of the territory in 1846.[6]

After Mexico took over the territory of New Spain in 1821, the settlement process in New Mexico was speeded up considerably. From the time Mexico as-

---

[3]Harold H. Dunham, *Government Handout,* New York: Edwards Brothers, 1941, p. 214.

[4]Coan, *op. cit.,* pp. 475-79.

[5]When the Spanish government was driven out of Santa Fe by the Pueblo Indians in 1680 almost all government records were destroyed including the territorial land records.

[6]Coan, *op. cit.,* pp. 475-79.

sumed jurisdiction over the territory in 1821 until the war with the United States in 1846, that Republic granted 30 petitions of settlers for land that were later confirmed by the United States. That there were many more grants allowed during the period there can be little doubt as many of the claims were never brought before the United States authorities for examination.[7]

Types of land grants: There were three types of land grants allowed by both the Spanish and Mexican governments. They were (1) the community grants given to a group of settlers or "community," (2) individual grants, given or sold to persons of some financial means, and (3) joint grants to a few individuals.[8]

Although the available evidence on the issue is limited, it seems that most of the Spanish and Mexican land grants were of the town or community type.[9] These grants were awarded to a group of petitioners who had banded together in order to better brave the dangers and privations of early pioneer life. Lands given to these settlers were of two varieties: farming

---

[7]Thomas Donaldson, *The Public Domain,* House Miscellaneous Document 45, 47th Congress, 2nd session, XIX. Washington: Government Printing Office, 1884, p. 406.

[8]Although these three types of grants are defined here, the attention of this paper is limited to the community type. The reasons for this are two. First, the majority of the original grants were of the community type. Second, with but few exceptions all grants in New Mexico eventually became community grants with the addition of new families of local origin or immigration. By 1854, when the office of the surveyor-general began hearings on land claims, and most of the information to be had on these grants became available, there was little distinction between the type of claims regardless of the original type it happened to be. For these reasons little attention is given in this paper to individual or joint grants.

[9]*Ibid.,* pp. 406-408, also Coan, *op. cit.,* pp. 475-79. It might be pointed out here that grants to Missions, Indian Pueblos, and military garrisons are omitted from discussion here since they were of an entirely different nature.

or irrigable land, to which the settlers were given titles for individual tracts; and common or pasture lands which were for the community to use in common "rich and poor alike." Land given to the towns or communities was called *realengos* or royal lands since the full title to the lands remained in the Crown and only the right of use and occupation was transferred to the people. In many cases, however, the individual grants of farming or irrigated land might be sold or otherwise disposed of after a certain number of years. (See Appendix). The early settlers in these towns or communities may have been of the ne'er-do-well kinds, although the quality seems to have improved during the later periods of Spanish occupation. As Blackmar has stated it, "the first settlers, though mostly Spanish, were of an inferior class, whose numbers were increased from time to time by invalids and discharged soldiers. But . . . the character of immigrants improved until the settlements were represented by some of the first families of Spain and Mexico."[10]

The joint grants in New Mexico were similar in many respects to the town or community grants. These grants were given to a group of families usually ranging in number from two to ten. The grantees in this case usually were responsible for financing the settlement venture although they might be given or loaned funds by the government to offset partially the costs. Families and individuals accompanying the grantees were given residential lots and a small portion of irrigable land to till. By and large, however, they fur-

[10]Frank W. Blackmar, *Spanish Institutions of the Southwest*, Baltimore: The Johns Hopkins Press, 1891, p. 186.

nished labor for the grantees who as a rule owned large herds of livestock.

Most of the individual land grants were issued during the early Spanish domination of New Mexico. These grants were usually distributed to individuals who assisted in conquering the country as rewards for their services. Some, however, were sold to individual buyers to help defray the expenses of current colonizing efforts. These lands were called *de dominio particular,* or private property, as the full ownership was usually transferred to the donees or purchasers.[11]

The proprietor of the grant was bound by certain rules and regulations with which he was forced to abide or else the land and its improvements would revert to the Crown. For example, usually he was required to provide some sort of government for the families brought with him. This generally consisted of an *alcalde,* most frequently the grantee himself, and a town council made up of the heads of resident families.

Spanish and Mexican Colonization Policy: The land laws of Spain were liberal in character, especially designed to induce colonists to settle the territory of New Spain. As mentioned above, not only were colonists allowed to settle on the land free of charge, but in many cases were paid to do so.

Under the Spanish "laws of the Indies" the ownership of all conquered lands in the "West Indies" belonged to the Crown. However, ownership was often sold to favored purchasers and the occupation and use

---

[11]Donaldson, *op. cit.,* p. 1126.

of the lands were transferred with little difficulty if with a great deal of formality.[12]

There were three types of lands recognized by the Spanish government in New Mexico. They were (1) the *consijiles* or lands assigned for the support of a town; (2) the *de dominio particular* or privately owned lands which had been sold or given to favored subjects; and (3) the *realengos* or royal lands were also known as *terrenos valdios* or vacant lands because nothing was paid for their use.[13]

The royal lands, obviously, included all but a small portion of the entire territory. All vacant lands were designated as *realengo* lands as were the commons or pasture lands surrounding each settlement. Use of these lands was granted the settlers to the extent needed for their flocks and herds, who accepted this privilege as a matter of course.

In the early years of settlement, petitions of the settlers for *realengo* lands were made directly to the king. This procedure was expensive as well as time consuming and a royal decree was issued in October 1754 making it possible to submit the petitions to appointed delegates residing in the territory.[14] This decree was instrumental in speeding up the rate of settlement in the territory.

Other royal decrees were issued in subsequent years relative to the disposition of the public lands, culminating in the decrees of 1791 and 1798 which made it unnecessary to apply to the political council for ap-

---

12*Ibid.*, p. 402.
13*Ibid.*, p. 1126.
14*Ibid.*, pp. 1126-27.

proval of any lands valued at less than $200 and gave
the local military captains authority to confer grants
within the vicinity of their garrisons. Under these
ordinances and modifications grants continued to be
made in the territory until the revolution of 1821 when
Mexico gained its independence from Spain and took
possession of the territory. Thus, in summary, it is
seen that:

the constant policy of Spain was to encourage by all means
the settlement of her possessions in the New World; that,
while the absolute ownership of the *realengo* lands was retained
by the Crown, laws from time to time were passed for the
purpose of enabling actual settlers to obtain titles to so much
of these *realengo* lands as they required for their use and
occupation in the pursuits of agriculture and stockraising;
yet, while the terms under which titles to these *realengo* lands
could be obtained for actual use and occupation were so
easy as to be within the reach of petitioners of humble means,
still the government guarded with jealous care their disposition by passing such laws as made it impossible for the vassals
of the king to acquire them for any other purpose than that
of actual occupation and use.[15]

The occupation of the territory by Mexico in 1821
resulted in few changes in the land laws or colonization
policies already existing north of the Rio Grande.
There were, however, two changes that are perhaps
worth mentioning. The first one, brought about in
1825, required that anyone desiring a tract of land
for grazing purposes or agriculture must submit the
petition to the Secretary of State. In the same year
the territory of New Mexico was opened to settlers
from foreign countries providing they "submit to the
laws of the country . . . and except for land embraced

15*Ibid.,* p. 1127.

with the twenty leagues bordering on a foreign country, or the ten leagues bordering on the seashore."[16]
This latter change was a departure from Spanish procedure which had prohibited foreigners from settling
in the area. With these two exceptions the settlement
policies of the two countries were the same.

Under Spanish colonization policy settlers were
"enlisted" in very much the same manner as if they
were being taken into the army. Prior to 1779 each
settler was equipped with all essential tools and equipment for farming and paid a small salary until he had
become self-sustaining on the land. Each settler was:

entitled to receive annually one hundred and twenty dollars,
with food for the first two years after enlisting as a colonist,
and provisions alone for the three following years . . . each
settler was entitled to receive a house-lot, a tract of land for
cultivation, another for pasture (commons) and a loan of
sufficient stock and implements to make a comfortable beginning. In addition to these, he received two mares, two
cows and one calf, two sheep, and two goats, two horses, one
cargo mule, and one yoke of oxen or steers; one plow point,
one spade, one axe, one sickle, one wooden knife, one musket,
and one leather shield.[17]

In 1799 this regulation was changed to give each
settler one hundred and sixteen dollars and seventeen
cents ($116.17) for each of the first two years and
sixty dollars per year for the next three years. If after
five years the settler had tilled the soil and made certain improvements on the land he came into possession
of an irrigated tract of land for life and the life of his
children. These regulations, obviously, applied only to

16*Ibid.*, pp. 1128-29.
17Blackmar, *op. cit.*, pp. 164-165.

the "enlisted" settlers as the large, private or individual grantees were responsible for their own families.

The degree to which this general Spanish colonization policy was executed in practice varied considerably in the different parts of Spanish colonial territory. There is little evidence to support the thesis that the policy was carried out literally with any degree of completeness in the New Mexican settlements.[18]

After Mexico gained her independence the practice of subsidizing colonization in the New World, as established by Spain, was continued with little deviation. Under the decree of 1825 Mexico allowed "an advance payment of transportation expenses, a living for one year after they have settled, farming tools and building materials for the construction of their houses; an acquisition of a determined tract of land for tillage and building purposes" and other miscellaneous items of household and farming equipage.[19] These inducements were also open to foreigners, who, in addition, were entitled to Mexican naturalization and citizenship papers. Foreigners were also exempt from payment of import duties on the goods and equipment transported into the territory.

Government of the settlements was specifically provided for by both the Spanish and Mexican governments. Although supreme authority resided outside the territory each *Pueblo* or settlement had its local government consisting of a minimum of an *alcalde* or may-

18A search through some thirty records of land grants in the General Land Office, Public Survey Office, U.S. Department of Interior, Santa Fe, New Mexico, failed to disclose any extensive gifts of livestock or equipment mentioned.

19Donaldson, *op. cit.*, p. 513.

or and a town council. The town council was elected
by the people and the *alcalde* was usually appointed
by the territorial government. The actions of both the
alcalde and council were subject to review by the government's representative at Santa Fe and often by the
captain of the nearest garrison.

Both Spain and Mexico required that the colonists
keep a vast assortment of fighting equipment in readiness to go to the aid of the Crown or Republic. Although few calls were made on the settlers for military
duty, their bows and arrows and muskets were frequently used to ward off attacks of the warlike Navajo
and Comanche Indians.

*United States Policy Toward the New Mexico Land
Grants:* The treaty of Guadalupe Hidalgo signed in
Mexico on July 4, 1848, brought to a close the war between the governments of Mexico and the United
States. It was agreed in this treaty that, for the sum of
$15,000,000, the Republic of Mexico would release
claim of all but a small part of the territory now covered by the state of New Mexico to the United States.
It was further agreed that all persons living in the territory, and electing to remain, would become United
States citizens and have full protection of their property rights "equally as if the same belonged to citizens
of the United States."[20] This obviously meant that all
bona fide claims to Spanish or Mexican land grants
would be recognized.

To cope with the many and varied claims to land in
the new territory the office of United States Surveyor-
General was created in 1854. One of the duties of the

---

[20]*Ibid.*, pp. 128-29.

Surveyor-General was to make an investigation of Spanish and Mexican grants and to submit his findings to Congress for approval or disapproval.

Soon after the establishment of this office claims of Spanish and Mexican titles began to pour in. By 1880 the office complained that since the establishment of the office "more than 1,000 claims have been filed with the Surveyor-General, of which less than 150 have been reported to Congress, and of the number so reported Congress has finally acted on only 71."[21]

The difficulties inherent in the task of the office of the Surveyor-General were many. Numerous grantees were reluctant to file their claims. Only a small fraction of the land had been surveyed prior to 1854, and on much of this the work was done none to accurately. Even after the claims had been acted upon by the Surveyor-General's office they had to be submittd to Congress for confirmation. This alone might involve a wait of two or three years. Donaldson sums these difficulties up in his statement that

there exist ancient Spanish titles, municipal and rural, claimed under the treaty of 1848 with Mexico, and what is known as the Gadsden purchase of 1853. These claims are for irregular tracts, illy defined, bounded by streams or marked by headlands, or natural objects in many cases since removed. They were made for agriculture, mining, stock-raising, or colonization, in all sizes from a village lot to a million or more acre tract. The records kept by the granting authorities of Spain and Mexico have been a serious hindrance in some cases toward a satisfactory solution, being frequently of doubtful meaning.[22]

---

[21]Ibid., p. 406.
[22]Ibid., p. 366.

As the task of reviewing and acting on all land claims proved too great a task for the Surveyor-General's office the Court of Private Land Claims was set up in 1891 to supersede it. Action was speeded up with this change and the land grant situation began to clear up. By 1904 the Court had acted on 301 claims, all but 75 of which were disallowed.[23] The total acres claimed were 34,653,340 and the total acres confirmed 1,934,-986.

Case Histories of Certain Selected Land Grants in New Mexico: In order to present a somewhat clearer picture of the nature and changes which have taken place in the land grants of New Mexico certain data are presented in the following pages on the history of four land grants. It is believed that the four grants selected represent, as well as such a small number could, the land grant situation in the Upper Pecos Watershed and that it sheds considerable light upon the state of affairs in the Spanish-American area as a whole. Each of the grants selected is (1) in the Spanish-American area, (2) was originally either a Spanish or Mexican grant, (3) was either a community grant or came into community ownership after a short time, and (4) was characterized by individual ownership of the irrigated land and of the grazing or pasture land in common.

1. *The San Miguel del Bado Grant:* The San Miguel del Bado grant is situated in the western part of San Miguel County. It was granted by the crown of Spain in 1794 to 52 families then living in the territory of New Mexico. In accordance with the natural boun-

---

[23]Coan, *op. cit.,* p. 477.

daries set down in the original papers the grant contained a total of 315,300 acres.[24] These boundaries included a tract of land on each side of the Pecos River, in San Miguel County, reaching from a point just above the present village of Anton Chico to a point just above the village of Upper Colonias.

The settlers took possession of the grant on March 12, 1803, settling at the present site of San Miguel. Under the direction of the Justice of Santa Fe the irrigated land was divided into strips of land measured from the river front. After this was completed the families drew lots for the portions they were to occupy. (See Appendix for details of occupation.) The pasture and grazing lands were to be held in common for use by all families.

Certain restrictions accompanied the grant and with these all the families were expected to conform. The principal obligations imposed were that (1) access must be given to settlers who might later come into the area and settle on the grant, (2) each family must have at least one bow with arrows and after two years all must have firearms, (3) a tract of land must be set aside for the *alcalde* or mayor of the town, and (4) the construction of the *plaza* irrigation ditches and other community works must be done by and with community labor. See Appendix.

Although the colonists were harassed somewhat by roving bands of Comanche Indians, the early settlement at San Miguel prospered financially and the population of the village increased. A Spanish population

------

[24]Donaldson, *op. cit.*, p. 1154. El Cerrito, the village studied, is located on this grant. See Figure 3.

census of 1827 gave the number of people living at San Miguel at 2,893, a number that may have been exaggerated.[25] A map of the state made in 1844 shows the location of La Questa, another village on the grant, indicating that the settlement had begun to branch out. By 1900 all ten of the villages existing on the grant today had already been established.

The first petition made to the United States for a confirmation of the San Miguel del Bado Grant was submitted to the office of the Surveyor-General at Santa Fe, New Mexico, on March 18, 1857. Here the petition remained until 1879 when the Surveyor-General submitted the petition to Congress recommending that only part of the grant be approved.[26]

Despite the request of the Surveyor-General that the petition be "speedily acted upon" by Congress there is no evidence that this august body ever considered this title and it was still an "unconfirmed claim" when the Court of Private Land Claims replaced the office of the Surveyor-General in 1891.

In 1904 the Court of Private Land Claims examined the claim, as well as the report of the Surveyor-General, but failed to allow most of the acreage embraced in the petition. This court reduced the amount to 5,024 acres, which is almost exactly the acreage which was designated as irrigable land.

Obviously, the people concerned as owners of the

---

[25]Coan, *op. cit.*, p. 325.

[26]Public Survey Office, *The San Miguel del Bado Grant,* Report No. 119, File No. 49, U.S. Department of the Interior, General Land Office, Santa Fe, New Mexico. The recommendation was for the approval of less than the full 315,300 acres. Attached to the petition is what was purported to be an original copy of the grant from the Crown of Spain.

grant were displeased with the decision; and they finally elected to appeal the case. To meet the necessary lawyers' fees and other costs of the appeal several of the stockmen on the grant sold large numbers from their herds and flocks of livestock. The appeal was denied. The claim still remains at a little more than 5,000 acres as it was surveyed in the year 1916.

As originally provided for in the contract with the Crown, the grant was to be administered by a Board of Trustees at first appointed by the Spanish Provincial government and subsequently elected by the people. This Board, consisting of five people elected each two years, is still in existence. Its chief duties are looking after the legal aspects of the grant, seeing that the annual taxes are paid, and arranging that any *bona fide* descendant of a grantee who comes of age is enabled to secure a residential lot. No more irrigable land can be distributed in this manner, since all of it has been long absorbed by the existing people in the different villages. As a result the land is now almost 100 per cent individually and privately owned.

2. *The Anton Chico Grant:* The Anton Chico Grant is located on the Pecos River. It embraces parts of southern San Miguel County and northern Guadalupe County.

This grant was originally given to a group of 36 persons by the Mexican government in 1822. According to the boundaries set down in the grant, the original claim embraced 383,856 acres.[27] The irrigable land in this grant was divided among the families who were to occupy the grant; and the other was designated as

27Donaldson, *op. cit.*, p. 407.

"common" land to be used in common by the settlement "as meets their needs." The government of the
village was to be by *alcalde* and town council elected,
as was the general practice, by the people.

Petition for confirmation of this grant was made
to the Surveyor-General in Santa Fe soon after that
official took office in 1854. After a brief examination
of the claim, which had been preserved by the grantees,
the Surveyor-General recommended that the grant be
approved. This was confirmed by Congress in 1860
although the acreage, after careful survey, was reduced
to 278,000.[28]

The population on the grant has increased slowly.
Anton Chico was still the only village on the grant in
1844.[29] As late as 1920 there were only three villages
on the grant, Anton Chico, Dilia, and Colonias. In
1939 the population of these villages totaled but little
over 700.[30]

The grant is still owned in community by the heirs
of the original grantees. It is administered by a Board
of five Trustees who are elected every two years.
During recent years the duties connected with the job
have consisted largely of keeping it leased to outside
stockmen and of seeing that the taxes are paid on the
"common" or pasture lands.

Although taxes on the irrigated tracts of the Anton
Chico grant are paid regularly, the taxes on the "common" or pasture lands frequently have been neglected
in the past. Since 1926 the problem of delinquent taxes

[28]Soil Conservation Service, Albuquerque, New Mexico. Unpublished data
on a survey of the Upper Pecos Project, 1939.
[29]Coan, *op. cit.*, p. 305.
[30]Soil Conservation Service, *op. cit.*

on the "common" lands has become a serious one. In that year the tax laws of New Mexico were revised to make land subject to foreclosure for taxes delinquent for three years or more. Beginning in that year part of the "common" land was sold in large tracts to outside stockmen. These sales have continued until, in 1939, only 80,000 acres of the original tract still belonged to the people.[31]

3. *The La Joya Grant:* The La Joya Grant is located in the northern part of Socorro County, New Mexico. It embraces a tract of land that is almost bisected by the Rio Grande River. Part of the area is irrigable but the main portion of it is not.

This grant was made by the Spanish government to a group of 67 families, in 1819. Like most of the other grants of that time the irrigable land was to be divided equally among the settlers and the pasture or grazing land was to be held in common by all. The terms of the grant specified that "they were to maintain houses and arms in readiness to defend the caravans and wagon trains against hostile Indians."[32]

The grant was confirmed by the Court of Private Land Claims for New Mexico in 1901. A survey at that time allowed the grantees a total of 272,193 acres.[33] It was required that the grant be managed by a Board of Trustees elected by the people. This organization is in existence at the present time.

[31]Soil Conservation, *op. cit.*

[32]Soil Conservation Service, *Notes on Community-owned Land Grants in New Mexico,* U.S. Department of Agriculture, Albuquerque, New Mexico, 1939, p. 20.

[33]Public Survey Office, *The La Joya Grant,* Report No. 95, File No. 169, U.S. Department of the Interior, General Land Office, Santa Fe, New Mexico.

The grazing lands of the grant have been in continuous use by large stockmen. At times these stockmen have been descendants of the original grantees and at other times they have been outsiders. At all times the grantees have been free to pasture any livestock they happened to have on the grant free of charge.

After title was confirmed for the grant no provision was made for the payment of taxes. By 1920 delinquent taxes on the grazing or "common" land aggregated approximately $23,000.[34] Realizing that something must be done to meet the demands of the county for delinquent taxes a tract of 10,000 acres was sold in 1921 for a total of $18,500. Although this sum of money was supposed to have been applied against the tax delinquency there is no evidence in the county records to prove that this was done and the people are very hazy about what happened to the money.[35] From 1923 to 1928 some taxes on the grant were paid but the total kept increasing by almost $5,000 per year.

In 1937 the grant was offered for sale by Socorro County for the delinquent taxes which, by this time, amounted to approximately $30,000. It was bought by Thomas D. Campbell, the so-called "wheat king" for $76,000 or about 35 cents per acre. Since this sale the people have been considerably agitated and have petitioned President Roosevelt to intervene and in some way grant them a loan with which they might redeem the grant.

---

[34]County tax records, Socorro County, New Mexico.

[35]Soil Conservation Service, *Notes on Community-owned Land Grants in New Mexico*, U.S. Department of Agriculture, Albuquerque, New Mexico, 1939, p. 23.

At the present time there are approximately 1700 people living on the grant most of whom are descendants of the original grantees.[36] As is the case for most of the villagers in northern New Mexico, the people living on the La Joya Grant have long been dependent on other sources than the grant land for their cash living. Most of the men are farm laborers doing seasonal work such as herding sheep, thinning and harvesting beets, and performing other farm work in the surrounding states of Texas, Colorado, Utah and Wyoming. However, they have clung to their small irrigated holdings upon which they depend heavily for food to supplement the cash earned in wage work on the outside.

4. *The Canyon de San Diego Grant:* The Canyon de San Diego grant is situated in Sandoval County, New Mexico, on the western slope of the Nacimiento Mountains. The Jemez River runs across the grant dividing it into two very nearly equal parts. The altitude of the lands in the grant is relatively high, varying in height from approximately 6,000 to over 9,000 feet.[37]

This grant was given by the Crown of Spain in 1798 to "the families residing in the vicinity of Jemez Springs."[38] In 1860 the Surveyor-General of New Mexico recommended that Congress approve the grant. This Congress did in the same year. The acreage, as confirmed, aggregated a total of 110,000 of common or grazing land and 6,000 of farming land the greater

---

[36]From copy of petition of the grantees to the President, 1938.

[37]Soil Conservation Service, *op. cit.,* p. 5.

[38]Public Survey Office, *The Canyon de San Diego Grant,* Report No. 25, File No. 60, U.S. Department of the Interior, General Land Office, Santa Fe, New Mexico.

portion of which was irrigable. This irrigable land was recognized as belonging to the individual families as provided for in the original Spanish decree.[39]

Until 1870 the "common" land was used almost exclusively by the grantees to pasture their herds and flocks of livestock. At that time, however, an outside cattle operator named Otero began to use the land in the grant as summer range for his livestock. Gradually this cattle man began to buy up the individual holdings on the grant, specifying with each purchase that with the sale of the individual holdings went the individual's rights to the grazing land. These purchases continued until his death in 1904. By this time he had begun to claim the entire tract of "common" land for himself and to use it as if it actually were his property.[40]

Soon after Otero's death, in 1904, the heirs of the original grantees brought suit in the district court to recover claim to the grant. Under the direction of an able lawyer the claims of the grantees were recognized by the court and the final decision allowed the grantees 80 per cent of the 110,000 acres. Half of this went to the lawyer who presented the case leaving the grantees possession of the remainder or 44,000 acres.

The court then appointed a commission of three men to determine the best method of dividing the grant among the heirs. This commission decided that, because of the difficulty of dividing the 44,000 acres equitably among the heirs, the tract should be sold in a single block and the proceeds divided among those

---

[39]*Ibid.*
[40]Soil Conservation Service, *op. cit.*, p. 6.

families that could establish valid claims to the grant. The tract was sold at public auction in 1908 at 45 cents per acre. This sale netted the grantees approximately $20,000 and the sum was divided equally among the 200 persons or families recognized as legal heirs.[41]

At the present time, in order to use the grant the heirs of the original grantees must pay a fee of 25 cents per cow per season and 10 cents per season for a sheep or a goat. A charge of 20 cents is made for each wagon load of firewood that is hauled from the tract. If the wood is to be sold the charge is slightly higher.

From 1922 to 1932 the New Mexico Lumber and Timber Company cut approximately 100,000,000 board-feet of lumber from the tract. Although the lumber operations on the grant decreased considerably during the subsequent years, they were continued on the tract until 1936. By this time the trees suitable for lumber had been almost completely cleaned out.[42]

During the period of extensive lumber operations mentioned above work was available for the grantees in the industry and at substantial wages. But with the dwindling of the industry more and more of the people were forced to search for employment on the outside. At present they are following seasonal farm work in New Mexico and surrounding states.

THE LAND GRANT IN ITS RELATIONS TO
SETTLEMENT PATTERNS IN EL CERRITO

The settlement pattern or manner in which the people are distributed on the land has long been recog-

[41] *Ibid.,* p. 8.
[42] *Ibid.,* p. 10.

113

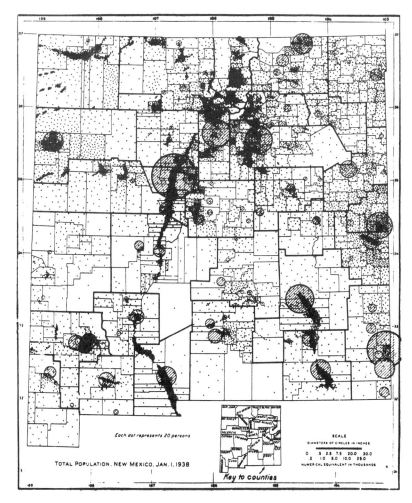

Source: Bureau of Agricultural Economics.
Figure 5. Distribution of the Total Population of New
Mexico, 1938.

nized as an important factor in the social life of farm folk. As Smith has said, "the manner in which the rural population is arranged on the land is one of the most important aspects of rural social organization."[43] If the farm houses of a rural people are clustered together social contacts are likely to be frequent and intimate. If they are spaced widely apart the opposite is likely to be true, other factors being equal.

New Mexico is one of the few states of the United States in which the clustered or village type of rural settlement is a significant part of the general pattern. Almost the entire Spanish-American population of the state is concentrated on the main streams and in small, agricultural villages.[44] See Figure 5 and Figure 2. This was the pattern dictated to all prospective colonists by the Spanish government which first opened the territory for settlement in 1598, and by the Mexican government which succeeded the Spanish Crown. As Blackmar has written, "there was, however, one distinct feature of the Spanish-American town which separated it from others . . . and that was unformity."[45] In each village or settlement the houses were grouped around the *plaza*. The irrigable fields were just outside the village and the common or pasture lands further beyond.

This pattern prevails today in El Cerrito. With the

[43]T. Lynn Smith, *The Sociology of Rural Life*, p. 201.

[44]The agricultural village is defined here as a village "the bounds of which are more or less definite, and in which the population is made up predominantly of farmers and their families." See Lowry Nelson, *A Social Survey of Escalante, Utah,* Brigham Young University Studies 2, Provo, 1925, p. 3.

[45]Blackmar, *op. cit.,* p. 161.

exception of three families, which have built houses out on the once commonly owned land, that they now farms, all houses in El Cerrito surround the *plaza*. Old *adobe* houses, barns, and sheds give ample testimony to the fact that little change has taken place in the settlement pattern of El Cerrito since the time most of the houses were constructed, nearly 100 years ago.

There is little doubt that the nature of the Spanish grant on which El Cerrito is located has been instrumental in perpetuating the original village pattern of settlement. The terms under which the Spanish grants were donated made it extremely difficult for an individual to move out on his own individual holdings unless he was in a position to "found a colony after prescribed rules."[46] These rules would make it necessary for him to take several families with him and establish a new colony.

The provisions of the San Miguel del Bado Grant, on which El Cerrito is situated, explicitly stated that "the tract aforesaid (grazing land) has to be in common." See Appendix. Consequently there was no opportunity for a family to move out onto its own holdings as was the case in the western expansion of the New England colonies.

The terms of the grant also stipulated that the irrigated land be distributed "to all who may occupy said settlement." See Appendix. This land, which in El Cerrito represents a potential of approximately 40 acres, was equally diivded among the few original settlers. Living in a clustered or village pattern on the irrigable land made for easy access to the individual

---

[46]Blackmar, *op. cit.*, p. 162.

tracts of land which were farmed intensively and also made possible access to the outlying grazing lands which were used for carrying on the more extensive livestock operations.

Although nearly all the "common" grazing lands of the people in El Cerrito were lost in the decision of the Court of Private Land Claims in 1904, the loss affected the economy of the village but little until 1916.[47] For many years use of the land remained unrestricted, since the disallowed portion of the grant had simply reverted to the Public Domain of the United States. In 1916, however, surveys of the Public Domain in the area were begun and the land surveyed opened to entry under the Homestead Acts of 1862 and 1877. A few of the El Cerrito families filed for homesteads in the area but most of those filed for, and subsequently granted, were soon sold to outsiders. The provisions of the homestead law required residence on the claim, and the inhabitants of El Cerrito were loath to leave the village and establish permanent homes on these tracts. Furthermore, none of the homesteads were capable of supporting a family unit. The scant grass covering on a 640 acre homestead, the largest acreage allowed, would support only a few cattle or sheep; and no adequate water supply was available other than the few streams in the area which were in large part controlled by the grants of land in the area which had been allowed. Thus the provisions of the original grants served to "fix" or "set" the settlement pattern,

---

[47]As pointed out previously, El Cerrito is situated on a part of the San Miguel del Bado Grant which was reduced in size by the Court of Private Land Claims in 1904 from over 300,000 to about 5,000 acres. See Public Survey Office, *The San Miguel del Bado Grant, op. cit.*

and this manner of arranging the population on the land has remained largely unchanged. Families in the village continued to farm their individual, irrigated holdings and either seek supplementary seasonal work outside the village or, in case they had retained a substantial herd or flock of livestock, graze them on the surrounding and once commonly owned pastures of the grant now leased from other owners.[48] By introducing and perpetuating the Spanish and Mexican tradition of the nucleated settlement pattern, these land grants have had a large share in determining the relationships between the people and the land in El Cerrito, the upper Pecos Valley, and, indeed, throughout all the southwestern part of the United States.

THE LAND GRANT, SURVEYS AND TITLES, AND LAND DIVISION IN EL CERRITO

Both the Spanish and the Mexican authorities used two methods of dividing the land among colonists. The "common" or pasture lands of the grants were characterized by "indiscriminate location" with metes and bounds as boundaries. On the other hand, the cultivated or irrigable holdings were measured according to the "riverfront pattern" where a number of *varas* were accorded each settler along the river or other stream.[49] Beginning at the streams these long, narrow strips of irrigable land stretched back, often to the tops of nearby mountains.

---

[48]Questioning of the people in El Cerrito revealed that only six families have moved from the village and taken up permanent homes elsewhere.
[49]For a discussion of these systems of dividing lands, see T. Lynn Smith, *op. cit.*, p. 239.

As indicated above, the bounds of the original grants were vague and indefinite. This fact made it extremely difficult, once the grant titles were presented for confirmation, for the courts to determine the actual acreage covered by the grants, and where the lines lay. In 1878 Senator Thurman, Chairman of the Senate Committee of Private Land Claims, in a letter to the Secretary of the Department of Interior, wrote that:

the fact that the majority of these grants were never segregated from the Public Domain by actual survey or measurement in the field under the Spanish or Mexican Governments, but bounded by natural landmarks without reference to objects known to our public land system, it is impossible for Congress to determine the quantity of land the claimants are seeking ... the claimants prefer to obtain a confirmation of their claim by metes and bounds without regard to quantity.[50]

The boundaries of the irrigable holdings were usually more definite. At the time the settlers were put in possession of a grant a representative of the provincial government divided the irrigated land among the settlers and measured the tracts according to *varas* along the river front. Around these tracts were to be erected "mounds of stone . . . so as to avoid disputes." See Appendix. Basing the surveys on the river front and the fixing of man-made markers, made this second mode of land division much less haphazard than the first.

The effects of the river-front pattern of land division is obvious in almost any Spanish-American village of New Mexico. The strips of irrigated land were us-

[50]Donaldson, *op. cit.,* pp. 1137-38.

ually narrow originally and the practice of further dividing them among sons and daughters, who inherit alike under Spanish-American custom, has reduced the strips in many villages to a few yards in width. This phenomenon is illustrated in Figures 6 and 7 which show the holdings in the Spanish-American towns of La Questa and Cerro respectively, two of the most extreme cases in the state.[51]

The difficulties of inducing the Spanish-American claimants of New Mexico to submit their land titles to the office of the Surveyor-General of the United States have been pointed out earlier. One of the main reasons for this seems to have been that the colonists attached little importance to the titles until the United States took over the territory. Donaldson wrote in 1884 that "with paper titles of grant land held by men and women, stored away in old boxes or carried about their persons, no one can form any estimate of the area yet claimed in New Mexico or Arizona."[52]

The effects of the indefiniteness of boundary lines and careless surveys, or none at all, characteristic of the Spanish and Mexican land grants account in large part for the extremely heavy loss of land by the Spanish-American grantees after the United States took over the territory. The careless way in which the deeds were preserved added to these difficulties. There is little doubt that the office of Surveyor-General, and later the Court of Private Land Claims, attempted to confirm all *bona fide* grants but lack of title papers, in-

---

[51]These villages are situated in the Spanish-American area of the state, just north of the village of Taos, county seat of Taos County.

[52]Donaldson, *op. cit.*, p. 406.

120

Source: Soil Conservation Service.
Figure 6.   Strip holdings of Land in the Village of La Questa,
New Mexico, 1940.

Source: Soil Conservation Service.
Figure 7. Strip holdings of Land in the Village of Cerro,
New Mexico, 1940.

definiteness of acreage in the grants, and disappearance of original boundary markers for the grants made the decisions in many cases largely a matter of opinion.

In view of the haphazard nature of the surveys, divisions, and care of papers, it is not surprising that long before the appearance of the United States on the scene the Spanish-American area of New Mexico had been involved in inter-village and intra-village conflicts over land. Some of these persisted long after the original cause was removed. They arose over boundary disputes; they persisted as a socially inherited feud. Until recently the people of El Cerrito were involved in one of these boundary disputes, which at one time, became so intense it resulted in the death of one of their residents and the wounding of several others.

Fortunately for the people of New Mexico the "floating land grant" typical of parts of the Spanish-American area never prevailed to the extent that it seems to have in other sections of the Spanish colonization territory.[53] This seems to have been in large part the result of the fact that fewer individual grants were given or sold in New Mexico than in other territories such as California. Some of the individual grants did "float" about to a certain extent, however, as in the case of the Maxwell grant, which, from time to time, threatened to displace several hundred settlers as a result of re-surveys and claims recognized by the courts.[54]

[53]The floating land grant was a term applied to a number of grants that kept changing, usually enlarging, their boundaries each time it seemed legally possible to do so. See Henry George, *Our Land and Land Policy*, New York: Doubleday, Doran and Company, Inc., 1911, pp. 39-40.
[54]Dunham, *op. cit.*, pp. 212-241.

The consequences of the Spanish land system of indiscriminate location and indeterminate surveys[55] are readily evident in the land belonging to the people of El Cerrito today. Grant land belonging to the villagers is spread out in a pattern much resembling the state of Texas. See Figure 4. In some respects it resembles "an amphitheater — the buildings (and land) occupy a low position . . . bounded by the surrounding hills."

However, the irrigated holdings of the El Cerrito people, with few exceptions, still retain the rectangular pattern which is characteristic of river-front land division. Due to division of these holdings, and then redivision from generation to generation, many of these holdings are now no more than a few yards wide. Some of them are so narrow that they are no longer fenced as a fence would make it extremely difficult, and in a few cases impossible, for a person to turn a pair of horses around in cultivating or plowing his holding. See Figure 8.

Titles to these strips of land have seldom been recorded by the people of El Cerrito. Instead, providing such titles exist, they are kept in trunks or boxes at home. Naturally many of them have become misplaced or destroyed. This carelessness with documents has contributed greatly to confusion in property rights.

The indefiniteness of location in the Spanish land system is a factor in the present inability of most of the El Cerrito families to estimate accurately the size of their holdings. The people know, fairly definitely, how many *varas* they have on the river-front and where the

---

[55]Smith, *op. cit.*, p. 243.

boundary markers are, but if asked about the acreage in their irrigated holdings, will give an estimate and qualify it by the stock expression *poco mas a menos.*

Thus the land situation as it exists in El Cerrito today, characterized largely by small irrigated holdings surrounded by grazing lands lost as a result of poor titles and indefinite boundaries, reflects to a substantial degree what has happened over the Spanish-American area of New Mexico and, to some extent, over the entire area of the Southwest. It is an example of what can happen when a system of accurate surveys, definite titles, and permanent bases for location are superimposed upon a system characterized by careless surveys or lack of surveys, ambiguous titles and indefinite locations.

THE LAND GRANT AND LAND TENURE IN EL CERRITO

Land tenure has been characterized as "a social relatioinship between the population and the land."[56] In this sense the term connotes the rights an individual or individuals may hold in the land and the manner in which it is held. Under this definition land tenure becomes one of the most important factors involved in the study of rural farm life.

As pointed out earlier, the Spanish and Mexican community land grants conferred title to the "common" or grazing lands to a group of families in common while the irrigable land was parceled out in tracts to individual families. The "common" lands were considered to remain under the full ownership of the Crown under Spanish authority and to the Republic

[56]Smith. *op. cit.,* p. 260.

after Mexican occupation. The irrigated holdings, on the other hand, might usually be disposed of by the owners after a specified number of years set down in the settlement contract. See Appendix.

This pattern of dual ownership of land prevailed in El Cerrito until 1904. In the contract of the original settlers with the Spanish Crown "the tract aforesaid (grazing lands) has to be in common, not only in regard to themselves but also to all settlers who may join them in the future." Title to the grazing lands was placed in the hands of the Board of Trustees and each family was given an individual title to a tract of irrigated land and a residential lot.

Under this system of dual ownership the people of El Cerrito developed a personal interest and attachment to the irrigated land that was never approached in their interest in the grazing lands. This observation is substantiated in the four case histories of grants given previously where taxes on the grazing lands were often delinquent but seldom on the irrigated land. Today in El Cerrito families that own tracts of the once common grazing land acquired under the homestead acts often have them mortgaged or will sell them, but none of the irrigated holdings carry any financial encumbrance.

Although the El Cerrito families were allowed equal use of the "common" lands, this seems never to have been the case. From the beginning of the settlement until the "common" land was surveyed and removed from the use of the villagers the land seems to have been largely used by two or three large livestock operators in the village. All other families provided labor for these livestock operators and perhaps grazed a few sheep or cattle for themselves.[57]

There is one case of farm tenancy in El Cerrito today. In this instance the tenant is a part-owner since he has his irrigated land in the village and approximately three sections of grazing land on the mesa. All the rest of the families in the village are farm-owners, or more accurately land owners, since they each have a title to a residential lot, and all but two, title to a plot of irrigated land as well.

Thus the traditional practice of making each family on a Spanish or Mexican land grant an owner of at least a small portion of land accounts, in large part, for the high degree of land ownership existing today not only in El Cerrito but throughout the entire Spanish-American area of New Mexico. This phenomenon has other connotations also which will be discussed in detail in the subsequent pages of this work.

THE LAND GRANT AND SIZE OF HOLDINGS IN EL CERRITO

The size and distribution of land holdings is an important factor to consider in any attempt to understand the social life of any farm people. Not only the economic status but the social status of a people as well is in large part determined by the extent to which

---

[57]Out of this situation grew the *partido* system of share-cropping sheep. Under this system the large sheep owners rent large numbers of sheep to small operators. Under the contract binding the parties the renter is bound to return a specified number of lambs each year (usually around 20 per hundred of a specified minimum weight) to the owner and is also obligated to return the same number of sheep as rented at the termination of the contract. The renter also agrees to bear all expenses incident to the keeping of the sheep. This system of renting sheep is practiced widely over the Spanish-American area of New Mexico. The fact that it is an old system is evidenced in its mention by Josiah Gregg, *op. cit.*, p. 122, as early as 1844.

the land is divided among the families, i.e., whether the ownership of the land is somewhat evenly divided or is concentrated in a few hands.

Although the size of the Spanish and Mexican land grants was limited by law to not more than eleven square leagues of land, this limitation was not effective in practice. Due to an absence of surveys the boundaries outlining these grants of land were frequently found upon accurate survey to enclose several times the amount prescribed by law.

After the United States occupied the territory of New Mexico the office of the Surveyor-General, and later the Court of Private Land Claims, were instructed to recognize the size limitation set down in Spanish and Mexican law but for some reason, that is not at all clear from the records, frequently these instructions were ignored.[58] The most flagrant violation of this limitation in the territory of New Mexico was in the instance of the Maxwell land grant which, when confirmed, contained well over a million acres.[59]. It was not at all unusual for a grant of more than 100,000 acres to be recognized. The San Miguel del Bado Grant, on which the Village of El Cerrito is situated, contained more than 300,000 acres in the original claim.

Evidence of the once vast Spanish and Mexican land grants still remains in New Mexico. In the predominantly Spanish-American area of the state today (the eight counties shown in black in Figure 2) the majority of the farms fall into the categories of either

---

[58]Donaldson, *op. cit.*, pp. 1121-1131.
[59]Dunham, *op. cit.*, pp. 212-241.

large or small farms. The 1940 Census of Agriculture shows that in the eight counties of New Mexico where the population was over 75 per cent Spanish-speaking in 1938, about 7 per cent of the farms contained 1,000 acres of land or over. On the other hand, 55 per cent of the farms in the area contained less than 30 acres. This figure would have been considerably larger had the Census counted all irrigated holdings as farms since many of the holdings of the Spanish-American families are less than three acres. In the village of El Cerrito the irrigated holdings averaged less than two acres. See table II.

Only two families living in El Cerrito in 1940 owned more than a thousand acres of land. See Table II. While the average acreage of grazing land, for the families reporting owned grazing land, was 172 acres, the median acres owned was only 42. Many of these tracts are so poor and inaccessible as to be practically valueless to the owners. The irrigated holdings also are pitifully inadequate. The average for all families reporting irrigated land owned was under two acres. Some of the holdings were no more than $\frac{1}{4}$ acre in extent.

Each of the 20 families living in El Cerrito in 1940 owned at least a residential lot and 18 of the 20 owned some irrigated land. See Figure 8. Over a period of years these holdings have tended to become concentrated in a few hands. As Figure 8 indicates, several families have acquired from two to three strips of this land while one family now owns seven.[60]

---

[60]These combinations have come about through inheritance. It is extremely seldom that these strips of land are sold.

129

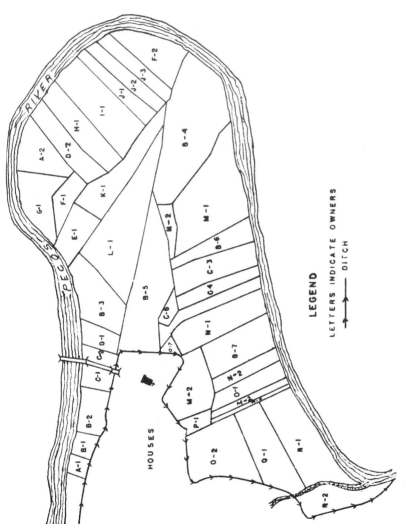

Source: Hydrographic Survey, New Mexico State Engineer's Office.
Figure 8. Irrigated holdings of El Cerrito People, 1940.

It should be evident from the data and discussion given above that the Spanish and Mexican land grants introduced a pattern of land holdings in New Mexico that still prevails to a great extent in El Cerrito as well as the Spanish-American area as a whole. The individual, irrigated holdings still are to be found in El Cerrito community and the Upper Pecos area much as they did during the Spanish and Mexican regimes. The principal changes in these holdings since occupation of the territory by the United States has been that they have grown smaller and come into the hands of a greater number of owners. The extensive common holdings, on the other hand, have largely been lost to the use of the Spanish-American population. In size and number many of them still exist but are now owned by outside and large-scale livestock operators who have come into the area and bought them as they were offered for sale.

This shift in the pattern of ownership has been a tremendous impact upon the economic and social behavior of the people affected. Some phases of this change will be discussed in the later pages of this study but it might be concluded here that significant social and economic adjustments are yet in process in the area as a result of the new restrictions in the use of the once commonly owned lands. As an example, the people are unable to understand why this land has been removed from their use, why they now have to pay a set charge even for firewood removed from the land. They have been unable to fully comprehend the significance of new barbed wire fences that literally enclose them in their small village holdings. Who owns the land, the people will tell you, doesn't matter but for an owner to restrict these lands to individual and private use is, for them, a new and extremely unpleasant experience. They are now caught in a situation in which their irrigated holdings are too small to provide a living, while the lands once used in common have become the private property of persons outside the village.

LAND GRANTS AS A CONDITIONING FACTOR IN THE RURAL
SOCIAL PROCESSES OF EL CERRITO

No analysis of group life can be complete without devoting some attention to the basic social processes by which life in the group goes on. In the following pages an attempt is made to isolate certain of the basic social processes in the village of El Cerrito and to point out how these processes have been conditioned by selected environmental phenomena, namely the Spanish and Mexican land grants.

1. *Competition, Conflict, and Cooperation:* Opposition and cooperation have been defined as the two fundamental forms of social interaction.[61] Out of these two basic processes arise all the others. Evidence of the functioning of each process is abundant in the Spanish-American area of New Mexico where an economy of scarcity has made cooperation expedient and an intimate and closely woven pattern of social contact has made conflicts inevitable.

The nature of the contracts accompanying the Spanish and Mexican land grants made cooperation

61Kimball Young, *An Introductory Sociology,* New York: The American Book Company, 1934, p. 348. See also T. Lynn Smith, *op. cit.,* p. 433.

between the individual families in a new settlement mandatory. There was always a certain amount of work stipulated in the contracts that must be done in common as "the construction of their *Plaza* as well as the opening of ditches, and all other work that may be deemed proper for the common welfare shall be performed by the community with that union which in their government they must preserve." See Appendix. This form of cooperation has been designated as "labor in common" and played a major role in the early life of the Spanish and Mexican colonies and to a considerable extent exists in the Spanish-American villages of New Mexico today.[62]

An example of this "labor in common" form of cooperation in El Cerrito is the "Ditch Association" an organization that has a history as old as the village itself. The function of this association is to clean the irrigation ditches once each year and to make any repairs that may become necessary during the year. This association is headed by a "ditch boss" who is elected annually to supervise any work on the irrigation system. The "ditch boss" does no work himself, his sole duties being of a supervisory nature. The actual labor is performed by the members of the association. All farmers operating irrigated land are members and must report for work at any time the "ditch boss" calls them out or else pay the group for doing their share of the work.

The informal aspects of cooperation in El Cerrito are much more pronounced than the formal. Through

---

[62]William F. Ogburn and Meyer F. Nimkoff, *Sociology,* New York: Houghton Mifflin Company, 1940, p. 345.

years of interdependence the people are conditioned to call upon neighbors and relatives for many types of assistance and, in turn, are expected to reciprocate when the need arises. Any task that requires greater strength or physical effort than a single family can supply is solved by calling in one or more neighbors. Many of the cooperative affairs almost have become social events as when several families are called in to help butcher a hog or erect the roof of a new house. It is not unusual for such events to be attended by far more families than could possibly be of assistance unless they work in turns. The village type of settlement which prevails greatly facilitates this type of mutual aid.

Any personal misfortune a family may experience in El Cerrito is shared, in so far as possible, by neighbors, relatives and friends. In case of serious illness there is never a lack of volunteer men and women to help. In case of death each adult in the village spends some time at the "wake" always given at the home of the deceased. There is a great deal of borrowing and lending in the village also and there is seldom a complaint for failure to repay these loans. This is true in the village although town merchants frequently point out that the reverse is true in their dealings with the same people.

The description of these cooperative activities could be continued at length. Here it is important to point out that the nature of the original grants and the settlement types established under their terms have been of great significance in perpetuating these cooperative activities.

There is also ample evidence to support the thesis that the nature of the Spanish and Mexican land grants have been a strong factor in promoting both intra-village and inter-village conflict. Disputes over grant boundaries, tendencies on the part of some few families to monopolize the grazing lands, water supply, and other resources have often developed that still persist in the Spanish-American villages long after the source of grievance has been removed. Representatives of various governmental agencies operating in the Spanish-American area frequently give examples where operational efficiency has been sacrificed in order to please existing village factions. For example, during recent years the Soil Conservation Service has endeavored to combine many of the small irrigation ditches into larger and more efficient canals only to find that the villagers refused to cooperate. Such combinations would make it necessary for strong intra-village factions to work together.

The history of one of these conflicts in El Cerrito well illustrates how intense such conflicts may become. The following story is as a resident of El Cerrito told it:

The village of El Cerrito was settled by the M's and my people (the Q's). They came in almost equal numbers, just about as many M's as Q's. Both families had some money and large numbers of sheep and cattle. At first there was no trouble between them. All were friends, although only one marriage ever took place between the two families. The M's used to herd their stock on the north side of the village and my people herded theirs on the south side. But as the herds kept getting larger the M's began to come into our territory. At first we didn't mind so much. There was plenty of grass and we didn't want to have any trouble with them. They were mean people. They were always getting drunk and fighting among themselves. Finally we had to tell them to stay out of our territory. This made them very angry and they began to do things to us. Sometimes they would take our calves and lambs and brand them with their own mark. Things got so bad between the families that they would not speak. Then fights began. Finally one of the M's hit my grandfather over the head with a shovel and almost killed him. My uncle ran for the sheriff but the M's followed him and almost beat him to death. This made my father very angry. He took his gun and shot one of the M's. He didn't die but he was sick in bed for a long time. There was a big trial after that which lasted for a long time. It was a very expensive trial and cost both families almost all the sheep and cattle they had. The M's were left in such bad shape that they all left the village, and our people were never able to get back their property.

Obviously, the statement that "because of its deep and lasting significance to life, land has been the cause of some of the greatest conflicts between nations of the world, and between the people within these nations" has been true for the Spanish-American area of New Mexico.[63] Such conflicts as that described by the resident of El Cerrito have all too often made the Spanish-American people easy prey for those who have been willing to take advantage of this weakness. So intense are many of these conflicts today that the participants would much prefer to lose their remaining resources rather than join hands and attack their common economic problems in unison. This situation has been one of the primary reasons why "the sturdy Anglo-Saxons over-powered and dominated the Spanish peo-

63Carl C. Taylor, *Rural Sociology,* New York: Harper and Brothers, 1933, p. 110.

ple, who long before migrated from the mother country; and now within the boundaries of the United States are slowly absorbing or crushing the last remnants of the institutions of this romance people. Today the Anglo-Saxon exults in the strength of a predominant and united nation, while the Spanish-American yet within our borders deplores the failure of his people, and reflects on the *'buenos tiempos'* of the Spanish occupation."[64]

2. *Accommodation, Assimilation, and Acculturation:* As it has been aptly put, "if social life has its conflicts, it also has its adjustments."[65] Such adjustments have not been lacking in the village of El Cerrito nor in the much larger Spanish-American area of New Mexico of which El Cerrito is a fairly typical segment. First, there were adjustments to be made as the result of coming into a nw physical environment and living in contact with a strange people, the American Indian. Later, the enterprising Anglo entered upon the scene bringing with him a new culture to which the Spanish-American today is still adjusting himself.

At the time of the Spanish occupation of the present state of New Mexico the position of the Spanish colonist in respect to the Indian was definitely one of domination. That which the Indian had and the Spanish conqueror wanted, be it land, goods or women, the latter took; and better firearms and more highly integrated forces were usually sufficient to make the acquisitions permanent. The Spanish-American taught

---

[64]Blackmar, *op. cit.*, p. 6.
[65]Ogburn and Nimkoff, *op. cit.*, p. 369.

the conquered Indian his religion, language and "the common arts, agriculture, and the practice of raising cattle."[66] On the other hand, he learned from the conquered Indian how to grow and use such crops as corn, potatoes, beans, squash, tomatoes, chili and others.[67]

With the arrival of the Anglo in New Mexico, however, the situation of the Spanish-American was reversed. Subordination and not domination came to gall him. No longer was he the conqueror but the conquered with all the usual implications that go with such a status. Under the impact of the contact with the aggressive Anglo the Spanish-American began a retreat to a position that has, from both an economic and social standpoint, become steadily more precarious. As Blackmar has summed up the land situation of the Spanish-American, "The original holders of lands have lost most of their holdings either through the misjudgments of the courts and commissions, or else by the wily intrigues of the Anglo-Americans, especially the latter. The Mexican has been no match for the invader in business thrift and property cunning."[68]

As in the case of the Spanish and Mexican colonists who borrowed heavily from their Indian predecessors, the Anglo too has adopted many elements of the Spanish culture. Blackmar, in his excellent work on Spanish Institutions, has listed some 35 Spanish words which have come into general usage in the Southwest.[69] Other borrowed traits are obvious to anyone taking a trip across the Southwest, including such items as:

---

[66]Blackmar, op. cit., p. 116.
[67]Smith, op. cit., p. 500
[68]Blackmar, op. cit., pp. 327-328.
[69]Ibid., pp. 271-279.

adobe construction buildings, Spanish architecture, a wide variety of foods and methods of preparing them, and many others too numerous to mention here. Above all, for the purpose of this treatise, has been the tendency on the part of large Anglo stockmen to take over the land grants given to settlers by the Spanish and Mexican governments as well as the original methods of operating them.

As pointed out earlier, the people of El Cerrito were but little affected by the change in government of the territory of New Mexico until the adverse decision of the Court of Land Claims in 1904 which took away their "common" or grazing lands. Actually, the full meaning of the decision was not realized until as late as 1916 when surveys of the land were begun and homesteads began to spring up all around them. When this situation was fully developed there was no alternative for the people but to rely on outside employment. Thus a pattern of seasonal work and seasonal migration began for these people which has continued to the present. Each seasonal work-peak will now find all but a few of the adult males of El Cerrito away from the village in one of the surrounding states.

With the increased contacts the Spanish-American people are having with the Anglo culture, brought about largely through employment, trade relations with the towns, and through the schools, it is obvious that the culture of these people is slowly breaking down. This fact is recognized by the people of El Cerrito as well as by the Spanish-American area as a whole. Many of the people are frank to admit that they would like to see the transition made as quickly as possible.

Actually there is considerable appreciation of the Anglo and his culture in El Cerrito. An Anglo family that once lived near the village is mentioned quite frequently and the farming practices of this family have been adopted locally to a limited extent. Many of the El Cerrito families stated a belief that the village would possibly benefit from having a few progressive Anglo farmers nearby. It would facilitate practice in the use of English and, some think, might afford an opportunity for the people to learn something of the techniques that have made the Anglos so successful in their push into New Mexico. It is admitted, however, that such a situation could be dangerous to the people's interests. Such families might manage eventually, to get possession of their remaining lands, a possibility that has become an actuality in many other parts of the state.

Although a satisfactory pattern of accommodation has been worked out between the Spanish-American and Anglo of New Mexico these two peoples remain separate and distinct groups. It is extremely seldom that the two groups intermarry and in the rare instances when this happens either the Spanish-American or the Anglo is taken into one of the groups and almost excluded from participation in the other. In summary, it might be said that a complete pattern of adjustment between the two groups has never evolved and will not until either a pattern of coercion and domination, or else equality, is generally recognized by both groups. Some of the factors that will enter into the adjustment have been discussed previously and others will be discussed in the subsequent pages of this study.

3. *Social Stratification:* The Spanish-American area of New Mexico is no exception to the statement of an eminent sociologist that "any organized social group is always a stratified social body."[70] Since the first group of Spanish colonists settled in New Mexico in 1598 a class hierarchy has existed that has ranged in height from Spanish noblemen to the lowly peon and slave.

During the early stages of Spanish colonization in New Mexico social stratification among the population was at its peak. At the top of the class pyramid were the few Spanish noblemen and officials who had bought or had been given huge tracts of land which they had pledged the Crown to settle. These grandees "were frequently men of high rank, in whose veins flowed the best blood of Castile. The old Castilian, showing disdain for the Mexican and his language, took great pride in his own language and pedigree."[71] At the bottom of the pyramid were the Indian peons or slaves who were under the "protection" of the grandees. In the middle layers of the pyramid were the "settlers" who had been given small tracts of irrigable land and large acreages of grazing land to pasture in "common."

Although the Spanish grandees and their progeny maintained their places at the top of the social pyramid until after the United States took over the territory, their places soon came to be challenged by a new type of grandee, a type that depended upon property,

---

[70] P. A. Sorokin, *Social Mobility,* New York: Harper and Brothers, 1927, p. 12.
[71] Blackmar, *op. cit.,* pp. 255-256.

mainly sheep and cattle, for a claim to social eminence rather than upon Castilian blood and a type of lisping Spanish.

This new type of grandee grew steadily in numbers. By fair means and foul his herds and flocks increased until, in most of the Spanish-American villages the "common" or grazing lands were being used by only a few families. Although many of the grantees would retain a few sheep or cattle most of the livestock became concentrated in a few hands. These big livestock owners were known as the *patrones* of the villages upon whom the majority of the other families depended for work.

With the coming of the United States into the territory, however, the *patron* as an important figure in Spanish-American life began to decline. He was no match for the Yankee in business deals and with the shift in ownership of the land base went the livestock enterprises of the *patrones*. With the exception of a relatively few who were shrewd enough to keep their resources intact or who had converted their resources into more lucrative channels the *patrones* lost out and became small farmers, merchants, or petty politicians.

The village of El Cerrito has passed through the stages of social change noted above. The older inhabitants of the village still remember the two *patron* families of El Cerrito one of which still lives among them. The people still talk of the vast holdings of these families and how they would entertain with elaborate *fiestas* and always provide work or provisions for the poor and needy among them. "These were the good old days," the people will tell you, "when we were prosperous and independent." Most of the people are hopeful that the government will some day return their lands and they will be able to live again as they did before the coming of the *Americanos*.

Although class differences still exist to a limited extent in El Cerrito, the bases of distinction have undergone change. In the first place economic distinction in the village is at a minimum. Only one family in the village owns and operates any significant amount of livestock and in this case only enough to supply labor for his own family and perhaps a few days of work to others each year during the peak labor season. Secondly, blood relationships in the village have become so widespread that almost any resident can claim at least a second or third cousin relationship to everyone else.

Thus in El Cerrito, as in the entire Spanish-American area of the state, the social pyramid has become somewhat flattened out. Such factors as age, family history, whether or not a man is a "good speaker" or clever politican are characteristics that carry some prestige value but, by and large, the people are *primos* and are of little social distinction one from the other. The exceptions to this are the descendants of the old grandees who claim to have remained apart from the rabble and maintained their Castilian blood, and children of the *patrones* who have managed to hold on to their property. A few of each of these may still be found in many of the Spanish-American villages and towns of northern New Mexico. By and large, however, the Spanish-Americans have become categorized as a group of small farm owners who maintain a sort of migratory existence traveling through the surrounding states following the seasons of farm work. Social differences among them are minimized, not only by the outsiders or Anglos but also by the Spanish-Americans themselves.

Thus the Spanish and Mexican land grants for many years operated to maintain an extremely peaked social pyramid among the Spanish-American population of New Mexico. With the rapid loss of these grants, however, there resulted an equally rapid decline in the height of the social pyramid. There is little doubt, however, that certain vestiges of the old class hierarchy still remain in the minds of the people. As an example, the old *patron*-laborer complex, although disappearing from within the Spanish-American groups, has been retained to some extent. The major difference between the new and old complex is that the *patron* now is usually an Anglo.[72]

4. *Social Institutions:* There is little doubt that the Spanish and Mexican land grants have been a major source of influence upon the institutional life of the Spanish-American people of New Mexico. The total extent of this influence in El Cerrito is beyond the scope of this paper but, in the following pages, an attempt is made to indicate some of the more obvious aspects of this influence upon three of the primary institutions of El Cerrito, namely, the family, the church, and the school.

As pointed out earlier, the nature of the land grants was conducive to the development and main-

---

[72]The transfer of the *patron* figure from the Spanish-American group to the Anglo group is discussed in Florence R. Kluckhohn, *Los Atarquenos,* Cambridge: Harvard University (Ph.D. Dissertation), 1940, pp. 13-24.

tenance of strong inter-village and intra-village factions. These factions usually had a family or blood
basis, a condition that was inevitable as a result of the
reluctance of the factions to intermarry. So strong
were the majority of these factions or "clans" that the
common pasture lands were divided between them
and to violate the recognized boundaries was equivalent to a trespass of private property under the New
England system of land use. Consequently, the two
factions, although living in the same village, had very
little social contact one with the other.

Within either one of these groups, however, common interests and social contacts were at a maximum.
The men worked together, either as laborers for the
patron or in tending their own herds or flocks which
grazed together. Under this consolidation of economic
enterprises, plus the tendency of the group to marry
within its own faction, there developed in time, all
over the Spanish-American area, a pattern of highly
integrated, extended or consanguine family groups.[73]
These larger kinship groups almost deserve to be
called clans.

The extended or consanguine family is characteristic
of El Cerrito today. Grandparents and grandchildren
are almost as intimately a part of the family group
as are the parents and children. It is not unusual for
one or two children of an immediate family to make
their home with grandparents or even a brother or
sister of one of the parents. Any older member of
these extended family groups is perfectly free to dis-

---

[73]Ralph Linton, *The Study of Man,* New York: D. Appleton-Century
Company, 1936, pp. 159-169.

cipline any younger member. Such authority is universally recognized and is seldom if ever questioned by either child or parent. This applies particularly to the female members of the family as the males are left to their own initiative at a relatively early age.

Conflicts as they exist for the people of El Cerrito are almost invariably between family groups rather than between individuals. This may be understood only in the light of the solidarity of the family groups. Infringement upon the rights of the individual necessarily means interfernce with the rights of the family and all members are prompt in responding to any threat to the individual's welfare. This phenomenon has been an important factor in prolonging many of the inter-village feuds in the Spanish-American area of New Mexico.

Until a comparatively recent date all marriages in El Cerrito were planned marriages in that parents and grandparents of the prospective bride and groom were always consulted. A primary object of this seems to have been largely a desire on the part of parents and grandparents to plan marriages in such a way that holdings of land and livestock might be combined most advantageously. This tendency, however, has declined markedly with the disappearance of grazing lands and the subsequent loss of the people's livestock. Today there seems to be little interference on the part of parents in marriages so long as the choice of a mate does not do harm to the reputation of the extended family concerned.

In the Spanish and Mexican colonization of the New World the State and Church worked hand in hand.

"The formula for the course of action of the crown
was exploration, conquest, unity of the church, acquisition of wealth, and the increase of the territorial
dominions of the king. The formula for the ecclesiastic
was — spiritual conquest, increased power of the order,
salvation of souls, extension of the king's domain, and
frequently, personal temporal blessings."[74]

In the establishment of either a Spanish or Mexican
colony, specific provision was made for the organization of the Church in the colony. Each settler was required to attend the church and to support it either by
contributions in money, goods, or labor. Failure on the
part of any settler to conform might mean his eviction
from the colony. The Church, in each instance, meant
the Roman Catholic Church since no other was toler-
ated by either the Spanish or Mexican governments.

The profound influence of the Church upon the
life of the people is still evident in the Spanish-American area of New Mexico today. In El Cerrito the influence of religion and the Church on these people
has diminished but little since early settlement. All are
devout Catholics. The influence of the Church is
found in their thinking, in their attitudes and values,
and in their day-to-day activities. Services are attended
regularly and in a humble spirit. Fees are paid prompt-
ly and special contributions are made periodically, if
meagerly. Although little money may be available for
food and clothing, a way is always found to obtain a
new costume for a child's first communion. The wom-
en are especially devout. When special services are held

74Blackmar, *op. cit.*, p. 53.

in the church, some of the men may remain away, but seldom does a woman absent herself.

The church is by far the most conspicuous and the best kept building in the village. Willing hands are always available should it need repairs or a new coat of whitewash. Holy Days are rigidly observed and Ascension Week receives special consideration and compliance. No work is done on these days because of the general belief that serious punishment from a Divine source would surely follow. The stories that tell of violations of Holy Days and subsequent retributions are numerous. For example, all in the village are familiar with the experience of a local farmer who, a number of years ago, plowed his corn on a Holy Day. The next day it was destroyed by hail. That the punishment was especially meted out to him is said to be proved by the fact that adjoining fields of his more devout neighbors went unharmed.

As prescribed by the early Church dignitaries in New Mexico the training of El Cerrito children in the knowledge and practices of the Church is begun at on early age. The child's first reading is often done from books on the catechism. Teachers in the school are especially esteemed by the parents if they are willing to help teach the catechism to the children. When a child has arrived at the age of ten he is expected to know the Church rituals and to be familiar with the teachings and practices of a good Catholic.

Neither the Spanish or Mexican governments encouraged or made provision for the formal education of colonists. Education was left to the Church, an institution which was opposed to popular education.

Schools in the Spanish-American area of New Mexico were virtually non-existent before 1890. Those which were in existence before 1890 were operated and controlled by the Church and the children were taught "religion, reading, riting, and reckoning, four r's instead of the three characteristic of the primitive school of the eastern colonies. Thus, between the formal rites of the church on one side and a life given over to the pleasures of the hour on the other, with enforced idleness on account of the services of the neophytes and lack of preparation for life by way of education, grew up a race of people not able, in educational and industrial zeal, to cope with the Anglo Saxons."[75]

This early disregard for the schools has carried over into present day El Cerrito life and thinking. There is little interest on the part of parents relative to the local school. Many parents consider what the children learn in the Church and from the teachings of the catechism as of far more importance than that which they learn in the school. Once the child has completed the eight grades offered by the local school there is no encouragement for the students to continue in school. Completing the *libro ocho* (eighth reader) is considered to be sufficient schooling to enable the student to speak and read a little English and master any work or skills the student is likely to use in his life's work.

Thus, it is obvious that the Spanish and Mexican land grants have affected the institutional life of the Spanish-Americans as well as their social processes.

---

[75]*Ibid.*, pp. 267-268.

Naturally, factors other than the land grants have also influenced the present day school, church, and family systems found in El Cerrito and other Spanish-American villages. However, it is also maintained that the influence of the land grant on the institutional life of these people is of such significance that it cannot be disregarded in any attempt to understand the social life of these people today. In fact, the nature of the land system, largely molded by the Spanish land grants, has in turn become one of the primary determinants of present-day institutional patterns.

5. *Migration:* Seasonal migration, or the movement of the people from one place and job to another, is a phenomenon that has only recently come to characterize the Spanish-American area of New Mexico. The original Spanish and Mexican land grants always provided ample land resources to enable the settlers to remain in one place, settled in a village, tilling their nearby irrigated holdings and grazing their sheep and cattle on outlying lands. With the loss of these lands, however, the sedentary pattern of life necessarily underwent drastic changes. The lands remaining in the hands of the people were inadequate to furnish more than a small portion of the things necessary to satisfy the needs of the people. There began an era of moving about searching for employment during parts of each year. This became periodic since the families always came back to their villages once the work season was over.

This pattern of seasonal migration in search of employment may have been adopted by the people of

El Cerrito somewhat earlier than in other parts of the Spanish-American area. When the Santa Fe Railroad began its line across the area around 1875, some of the people of El Cerrito, living very near the main line, began to work as day laborers for the railroad. Others furnished ties which could be cut from the timber on their "common" grant land. This work proved to be fairly steady for several years and the pay was considerably above that which a worker could earn herding sheep. By the time the road was finished, around 1890, the people returned to the land. However they remained there only about fifteen years, because, as has been indicated, the decision of the Court of Private Land Claims turned their "common lands" into Public Domain.

With the loss of title and use of their "common lands," which did not become apparent until around 1916, there was no alternative but for the men again to seek work outside the village. Their experience in herding sheep enabled them to secure work for large livestock concerns not only in other parts of New Mexico but in surrounding states as well. Other sources of employment were in the beet fields of Colorado, Wyoming, and Utah; some of the men were able to secure somewhat better pay in the employ of mine and smelter companies in these same states.

Once begun, this type of work continued until the depression of the 30's made it extremely difficult to secure work anywhere. Each year the men would leave the village *en masse* to be gone for periods as long as six or nine months without coming home. As a rule

the women and children would be left at home where
they could till the irrigated holdings of the families
and care for the livestock. With the money thus earned in outside employment plus the food produced at
home a family could live at about the same level as
in the past.

One of the most interesting observations on the
extensive seasonal migrations of the Spanish-American
people of New Mexico is the tendency of the small,
irrigated holdings in the villages to pull the migrants
back to their homes once the season of outside work
is completed. Families in El Cerrito frequently com-
ment on opportunities they have had to remain away
from the village permanently but only a few have ever
taken advantage of such opportunities. This "pull" of
the land has created something of a paradoxical situation in the village of El Cerrito, as well as in the Spanish-American area as a whole — an extremely mobile
adult male population offset by an intensely stable or
sedentary family population.

6. *Social Mobility:* During the Spanish occupation
of New Mexico social stratification of the population
was at its peak. Strains of royal blood, special honors
conferred upon selected officials created social distances between families and other groups that were
readily apparnt to all. Social distinctions prevented the
man of Castilian blood from associating socially with
the lowly peon or the government sponsored colonist.
These social distances were universally recognized and
seldom violated. To a considerable extent these differences in class also were of a caste nature. There was no
channel or ladder by which the peon could climb into

the ranks of the privileged group. Once established the ranks tended to prevail generation after generation.

Later, with the rise of the *patron* class among the Spanish-Americans, however, the channels of circulation between the layers of the social pyramid became more open and the caste element became of less importance. A man with some ingenuity and business acumen might rise within a few years from the laboring class to the exalted status of a *patron*. Economic position came to be a dominant factor in social status. With the development of this class and the accompanying decline of the nobility, the social pyramid of the Spanish-American population slowly began to flatten out. This flattening process was accelerated with the passing of time by the tendency of the residents of a village to intermarry. This change was concomitant with the rise of the *patron* class, since there was less reluctance on the part of the *patron* and his family members to marry outside their economic and social class than had been true for the older nobility.

With the coming of the Anglos into New Mexico the social pyramid of the Spanish-Americans underwent another radical change. The Anglo cared little for the existing class hierarchy and social distinctions. To him a person that spoke Spanish was a "Mexican," and it made no difference whether he was a *patron* or a sheepherder. Much of the existing ill feeling between the two groups dates from the time when the incoming Anglo dubbed the Spanish-American as "Mexican" and was called *"gringo salado"* in return.

In the history of El Cerrito may be traced the change in social mobility that has taken place over the entire Spanish-American area. Older residents of El Cerrito remember the time when the *patrones* of the village occupied a position of extreme power and prestige. But, with the loss of the resources of the *patrones* went the power and prestige associated with them. In present day El Cerrito the social pyramid is about as flat as it could be. Kinship ties between almost all the families plus common membership in all the social groupings have removed most of the basis for group and family distinction. Only the few families which are not related to the main family grouping of El Cerrito might be considered as at a slightly lower social level and there is no restriction to their marrying into the main family group.

The channels of social mobility outside the village of El Cerrito are seldom used. As pointed out earlier, a certain amount of college work would make it possible for a resident of El Cerrito to do professional work or service outside the village but this has rarely happened. Poor local schools and the poverty of the people make it extremely difficult for a young person to secure the substantial amount of education which would be necessary in order for him to move up the social pyramid in the outside world. Even should this be accomplished he must associate almost entirely with his own people since the associations between Anglos and the people of El Cerrito, as well as the Spanish-American people as a whole, are always at a minimum.

Thus, the people of El Cerrito, and the majority of Spanish-Americans in all New Mexico, literally have become enclosed, first, by a wide expanse of land owned and fenced by outside interest and, secondly, by an alien culture whose carriers have always considered themselves superior to the "Mexicans." These two factors have driven the Spanish-American people back into their last stronghold — their small village with its individually owned, small, irrigated holdings. Here, for the past few decades, they have been able to maintain themselves in a fashion discussed in previous pages. How much longer they will be able to hold out, unless relieved in some manner from the outside, is a problem confronting not only the Spanish-American people themselves, but every agency interested in the welfare of the area.

CHAPTER

VI

SUMMARY AND CONCLUSIONS

I N THIS STUDY an attempt has been made to determine the nature and importance of the Spanish and Mexican land grants as a factor influencing the social organization and processes of the Spanish-American settlements in northern New Mexico. A great deal has been written on the economic importance of the land grants in the Southwest but little attention has ever been given to the social significance of these grants to the people living on them.

Both the Spanish and Mexican authorities were liberal in the distribution of their western lands but the system of distribution used placed many restrictions upon the settlers occupying the land. Most of the land distributed was allocated for the common usages and not given in fee simple to individuals. To facilitate this common use special provisions were always made for its common maintenance and improvement. Since the Church and State worked hand in hand in all colonization, possession and use of the land grants by the colonists were dependent upon compliance with religious requirements and support of the Church. In addition to these specific regulations laid down by the authorities, the nature of the grants themselves was an important factor in shaping the social life of the people

155

in the Spanish-American area. The extensiveness of the grants, their common possession and use, indefiniteness of their surveys, boundaries, and titles have combined to produce an economic and social situation in the Spanish-American area that is entirely different from what might be thought of as representative, American rural life.

In order to determine some of the social influences of this land system and its subsequent changes on the people affected, the village of El Cerrito, New Mexico, was chosen for intensive study and analysis. In choosing the village four main criteria were set up as the basis for making the selection. They were (1) it must be entirely Spanish speaking, (2) it must be situated on an original Spanish or Mexican land grant, (3) it must be a definite part of the larger Spanish-American area, (4) it must be sufficiently isolated from main highways or larger towns that it would not have been influenced by them unduly. It is believed that El Cerrito meets these criteria of selection satisfactorily.

After selecting El Cerrito for intensive study the writer spent approximately seven months in the village, gathering a wide range of information and materials on the land situation and the people. An attempt was made to participate in the life of the village as far as possible. It is believed this was accomplished as nearly as it could possibly be done by an outsider.

The history of the village proved to be an abstract of the Spanish-American area as a whole. It was part of a large land grant given to the people by the Crown of Spain in 1794. Here the people had been living since little past 1800, pasturing their herds and flocks on the "common" or grazing lands and farming the small, irrigable tracts of land in the valley. Title to the "common land" was held by a special Board of Trustees elected by the people. Families held their own titles to residential lots and plots of irrigable land. With the coming of the American land system into the area, however, the situation underwent rapid change. "Common lands" which had been in use by the people for almost a century were turned into Public Domain. Families were left with only their irrigable holdings which were inadequate for more than a home site and a good-sized garden.

With this information of El Cerrito land and people in mind an attempt was made to discover some of the factors in the nature and history of the land grants that had been instrumental in bringing the situation in El Cerrito, and incidentally the entire Spanish-American area, about. Some of the major findings and conclusions may be summarized as follows:

1. *Settlement Pattern:* One of the most distinguishing features of the Spanish-American area of New Mexico is the tendency of the rural people to live in a village or clustered type of settlement. This pattern of settlement was made mandatory by both the Spanish and Mexican colonization authorities in the grants of land which they gave. Living closely together was conducive to operating the small, individually owned, irrigable tracts of land and also fostered cooperation in utilizing the "common" or pasture lands at some distance from the village. Subsequent loss of the "common" or pasture land has had little effect on the old pattern of settlement. Opportunities for the families to

move out of the village onto patented land have been minimized by the tendency of large tracts of land to remain intact with shifts in ownership. In addition, the owners of irrigated land have been reluctanct to leave without assurance of something as permanent elsewhere. Thus throughout much of New Mexico today, the village form of settlement still prevails, a heritage from the Spanish system of settlement and granting of land.

2. *Surveys, Titles, and Land Division:* A lack of accurate surveys, ambiguous and imperfect titles, a system of land division based on metes and bounds, all characteristic of both Spanish and Mexican land systems, today are a constant plague to the people of New Mexico. Before the arrival of the Americans in New Mexico these phenomena had occasioned numerous conflicts and disputes, some having persisted in the Spanish-American area until today. After the arrival of the Anglos, with a new system of surveys, titles and land division, the difficult problem arose of imposing a new land system over the old one. The result has been endless confusion, and in the end an enormous loss of land by individuals, families, and entire villages. In El Cerrito, as well as in the entire Spanish-American area, the people have been able to retain little more than the irrigated tracts to which they could prove individual ownership. The lands formerly held in "common" generally have passed into the private ownership of outside people and corporations.

3. *Land Tenure:* The fact that both Spanish and Mexican land grants made specific provision for each colonist to own some land, accounts, in large part, for

the high percentage of land ownership among the Spanish-American population today. These grants are also responsible for the fact that most of these holdings are extremely small, much too limited in size to produce more than a part of the food needs of the people concerned.

4. *Size of Holdings:* The extensiveness of the land grants in northern New Mexico has been a strong factor in preventing the rise of a large number of middle sized holdings in th area. These grants were originally conducive to the development of a few large livestock operations which dominated the grazing lands and employed the bulk of the remaining families as laborers. This pattern has changed but little since the loss of the grant lands to the Spanish-American people. Many of the grants allowed by the United States courts were bought from the original grantees for taxes; others that were converted to the Public Domain soon came into the hands of outside interests, either through consolidation of purchases or through leases from the State. Small, irrigated, and individually owned tracts of land, however, have remained in the possession of a large number of owners. Thus, since early Spanish occupations of New Mexico, size of land holdings in northern New Mexico has been characterized by one of two extremes, large holdings for the use of a few families and numerous small holdings for the use of the remainder.

5. *Competition, Conflict and Cooperation:* The land grants of New Mexico have been the source of both conflict and cooperation among the Spanish-Americans. Inter-village and intra-village conflicts

arose through frequent disputes over rights involving use of the land. Trespass was made easy by the lack of fences or even knowledge of where the real grant boundaries were. Once begun, such conflicts frequently developed into open feuds which lasted long after the source of conflict had been removed. On the other hand, cooperation between the "in-groups" of the area was pronounced. All work of a community nature was done through contributions of labor and usually with a minimum of friction. Vestiges of this early and extensive cooperation still remain in El Cerrito and the same thing is true for the majority of the other villages within the entire Spanish-American area.

6. *Accommodation, Assimilation, and Acculturation:* The nature of the Spanish and Mexican land grants, in their wide expanse of territory, concentrating the settlers in clusters and excluding everyone else, has obviously retarded the functioning of these social processes among the Spanish-American population of New Mexico. Situated in widely dispersed and inaccessible spots of the state, miles from any sort of modern transportation, the people of the Spanish-American area have literally been out of contact with the rest of the world. Some of the mechanical evidences of this isolation today may be found in the people's poor mastery of the English language and their lack of regard for or interest in popular education. Briefly, this isolation from other peoples has resulted in the maintenance of old Spanish culture in the area to such an extent that an Andulusian of 18th century Spain would probably feel much at home in a village such as El Cerrito today.

7. *Social Stratification:* During the early Spanish occupation of New Mexico the social pyramid among the people was highly peaked. At the top of the pyramid was a small group of families which enjoyed the special favor of the Spanish Crown. At the bottom of the pyramid were the peons and just above them the government sponsored colonists. By 1821, the beginning of the Mexican domination of New Mexico, the nobility had all but disappeared and their place had been taken by a new group of *patrones* who monopolized the livestock industry of the state. This group persisted until after the American occupation of the territory in 1846 and have not entirely disappeared today.

With the arrival of the Anglo, however, the social pyramid of the Spanish-American group rapidly began to flatten out. Part of this was due to the loss of resources by the *patrones* and part to the failure of the Anglo to recognize the existing class hierarchy. As a result of these factors, plus a constant tendency of the *patron* families to marry outside their own group, class distinctions between the Spanish-Americans were reduced to the extent that the status of the *patron* was little higher than that of the laborer who once had worked for him. Today there are few class or family distinctions in El Cerrito and, with few exceptions, the same thing could be said of all villages in the entire Spanish-American area of the state.

8. *Social Institutions:* The Church and the State went hand in hand in the conquest of New Mexico. Each was dependent upon the other and the strength of the combination prevailed over all resistance from

the idigenous people as well as the colonists who came in to occupy the conquered territory.

The division of labor between the two powers gave the Church the responsibility for the moral and intellectual upbringing of the colonists. As a result popular education was neglected although the teachings of the Church were well provided for throughout the Spanish and Mexican territory of occupation. Each land grant given to settlers made specific provision for incorporating the people into the Church although no provision was ever made for the building or maintenance of schools. Evidence of this emphasis is obvious in El Cerrito today. Each family attends church services regularly and supports the Church financially as far as its budget will allow, while little interest is evidenced in the support and teachings of the school.

The influence of the land grant on the Spanish-American family has been profound. As the result of common interests in grant lands and a tendency on the part of spatially proximate families to intermarry there has developed in the Spanish-American area a type of extended or consanguine family. In these families are included grandparents, grandchildren and brothers and sisters who are almost as intimate a part of the family as are the parents and children. In El Cerrito, and many other villages of the Spanish-American area, one of these intimate blood groups includes the majority of all the families in the settlement.

9. *Migration:* When the "common lands" of the Spanish and Mexican land grants were ample in extent for the demands of the occupants there was little need or opportunity for the people to move about from one

place to another. With the loss of these lands, however, the men of the Spanish-American villages were forced to leave their homes for parts of each year to seek employment. Most of this work has been supplied by the beet fields and livestock industries of the surrounding states, enterprises which require supplementary labor during peak seasons. During the spring and fall seasons of each year the men of the Spanish American villages leave their homes returning after the seasonal work is completed. Meanwhile the women and children remain at home tilling the irrigated lands of the village which supply a limited amount of food to supplement what can be bought with the men's cash earnings. This pattern of migration is highly uniform throughout the entire Spanish-American area.

10. *Social Mobility:* The New Mexico land grants, under the Spanish and Mexican regimes, were conducive to the maintenance of considerable social distance between different family and other groups among the Spanish-American population. With the rise of the *patron* class, however, a class based on property rather than ancestry, the channels for social mobility became more open. The attitude of the Anglo toward the Spanish-American class hierarchy and the tendency of the *patron* class to marry outside their own group both acted to break down the barriers of class distinction.

Today in El Cerrito, as well as in the Spanish-American area as a whole, class distinctions are at a minimum. Although there remain a few Spanish-American families in the *patron* class, by and large, there are no major class divisions. Social distinctions are now made much more on the basis of such factors as age and political acumen than upon property holdings or claims to royal blood or favor. Marriages in the area have come to be based much more on individual likes than upon class or family background.

APPENDIX

The documents in this Appendix were taken from the files of the General Land Office, Public Survey Office, U.S. Department of the Interior, Santa Fe, New Mexico.

165

APPENDIX

ORIGINAL PETITION FOR THE SAN MIGUEL DEL BADO LAND GRANT —

A TRANSLATION

I, Lorenzo Marquis, resident of this town of Santa Fe, for myself and in the name of 51 men accompanying me, appear before your excellency and state that, in consideration of having a very large family, as well myself as those accompanying me, though we have some land in this town it is not sufficient for our support, on account of its smallness and the great scarcity of water, which owing to the great number of people we cannot all enjoy, wherefore we have entered a tract of land on the Rio Pecos, vacant and unsettled, at the place commonly called El Vado, and where there is room enough, not only for us, the 51 who ask it, but also for everyone in the province not supplied. Its boundaries are on the north the Rio de la Baca from the place called the rancheria to the Agua Caliente, on the south the Canon Blanco, on the east the Cuesta with the little hills of Bernal, and on the west the place commonly called the Gusano — which tract we ask to be granted us in the name of our Sovereign, whom may God preserve, and among these 51 men petitioning are 13 Indians, and among them all there are 25 firearms, and they are the same persons who appear in the subjoined list, which I present in due form, and we unanimously and harmoniously as one person do promise to enclose ourselves in a plaza well fortified with bulwarks and towers, and to exert ourselves to supply all the firearms and ammunition that it may be possible for us to procure. And as we trust in a compliance with our petition we request and pray that your Excellency be pleased to direct that we be placed in possession, in the Name of his Royal Majesty our Sovereign, whom may God preserve, and we declare in full legal form that we do not act with dissimulation.

Lorenzo Marquis
For himself and the Petitioners

ORIGINAL DECREE FOR THE SAN MIGUEL DEL BADO LAND GRANT –

A TRANSLATION

On the 26th of the month of November, One Thousand Seven Hundred and Ninety-four, I, Antonio José Ortiz, Captain in the militia and principal alcalde of the town of Santa Fe, in pursuance of the order of Lieutenant Colonel Fernando Chacon, Knight of the Order of Santiago and civil and military Governor of this kingdom, before proceeding to the site of El Vado, I, said principal alcalde, in company with two witnesses who were Xavier Ortiz and Domingo Santiestevan, the 52 petitioners being present, caused them to comprehend the petition they had made, and informed them that to receive the grant they would have to observe and fulfill in full form of law the following conditions:

First—That the tract aforesaid has to be in common, not only in regard to themselves but also to all settlers who may join them in the future.

Second—That with respect to the dangers of the place they shall have to keep themselves equipped with firearms and bows and arrows in which they shall be inspected as well at the time of settling as at any time the alcalde in office may deem proper, provided that after two years settlement all the arms they have must be firearms, under the penalty that all who do not comply with the requirement shall be sent out of the settlement.

Third—That the plaza they may construct shall be according as expressed in their petition, and in the meantime they shall reside in the Pueblo of Pecos where there are sufficient accommodations for the aforesaid 52 families.

Fourth—That to the alcalde in office in said pueblo they shall set apart a small separate piece of land for him to cultivate for himself at his will, without their children or successors making any objection thereto, and the same for his successor in office.

Fifth—That the construction of their Plaza as well as the opening of ditches, and all other work that may be deemed proper for the common welfare shall be performed by the community with that union which in their government they must preserve.

And when this was heard and understood by each and all of the aforementioned persons, they accordingly unanimously responded that they understood and heeded what was communicated to them. Wherefore, I took them by the hand and announced in clear and intelligible words that in the name of His Majesty (God preserve Him) and without prejudice to the Royal interest or that of any third party. I led them over said lands, and they plucked up grass, cast stones and shouted "Long Live the King," taking possession of said land quietly and peaceably, without any objection; pointing out to them the boundaries, which are, on the North the Rio de la Baca from the place called the Rancheria to the Agua Caliente, on the South the Canon Blanco, on the East the Cuesta with the little hills of Bernal, and on the West, the place commonly called the Gusano, notifying them that the pastures and watering places are in common.

And that in all time it may so appear, I, acting by appointment, for want of a notary, there being none in this jurisdiction, signed this with my attending witnesses, with whom I act, to which I certify.

Antonio José Otriz

THE SAN MIGUEL DEL BADO LAND GRANT
— A TRANSLATION

(SEAL)

At this place, San Miguel del Bado, del Rio de Pecos, jurisdiction of the Capitol town of Santa Fe, New Mexico, on the 12th day of March, in the present year, One Thousand Eight Hundred and Three, I, Pedro Bautista Pino, Justice of Second Note of the Town of Santa Fe and its jurisdiction by verbal order of Colonel Fernando Chacon, Governor of this Province, have proceeded to this said settlement for the purpose of distributing the lands which are under cultivation, to all the individuals who occupy said settlement, and having examined said settlement and having examined the aforesaid cultivated land, I measured the whole of it from North to South and then proceeded to lay off and divide the several portions with the concurrence of all the parties interested, until the matter was placed in order, according to the means myself and the parties interested deemed the best adopted to the purpose, in order that all should be satisfied with their possessions although said land is very much broken on account of the many bends in the river, and after the portions were equally divided in the best manner possible, I caused them to draw lots, and each individual drew his portion and the number of varas contained in each one portion was set down, as will appear from the accompanying list, which contains the number of the individuals who reside in this precinct, amounting to the number of 58 families, between whom all the land was divided, excepting only the portion appertaining to the Justice of the Precinct, as appears by the possession given by the said Governor, and another surplus portion which by the consent of all is set aside for the benefit of the blessed souls in Purgatory, on condition that the products are to be applied annually to the payment of free masses, the certificates for which are to be delivered to the Alcalde in the office of said jurisdiction. And after having made the distribution I proceeded to mark out the boundaries of said tract from North to South, being on the North a hill situated at the edge of the river above the mouth of the ditch which irrigates said lands, and on the South the point of the hill of Pueblo and the valley called Temporales, a large portion of land remaining to the South, which is very necessary for the inhabitants of this town who may require more land to cultivate, which shall be done by the consent of the Justice of said town, who is charged with the care and trust of this matter, giving to each one of those contained in the list the amount he may require and can cultivate, and after having completed all the foregoing I caused them all to be collected together and notified them that they must each immediately erect mounds of stone on the boundaries of their land so as to avoid disputes, and I also notified them that no one was privileged to sell or dispose of their land until the expiration of ten years from this date, as directed by said Governor who, if he is so pleased, will certify his proper approval at the foot of this document, of which a copy shall remain in this town and the original be deposited in the Archives where it properly belongs.

Pedro Bautista Pino
(By order of the Governor)

HOME REMEDIES
USED IN THE VILLAGE OF EL CERRITO

Stomach Cramps—Eat the leaves of a native mint plant (Yerba de la negrita). Also, a spoonful (teaspoon) of camphor in a tumbler of water and drink.

Fainting—Cut an onion in half and place the parts, alternately, under the person's nose. The aroma will revive him. In addition to this, wash the face of the person with cold water.

Sorethroat—A few drops of HHH medicine in water and gargle. Baking soda also good mixed with a little sulphur.

Sores—Wash well with salt water and then apply dust found inside the bark of *sabina* (juniper) post.

Earache—Put a little perfume in the ear. Also, urine of a healthy child.

Falling hair—Boil the roots of a gourd plant and wash with it. Wash hair in fresh, warm cow urine.

Freezing—Rub the affected part with onion.

Headache—Apply vinegar on sides of head and forehead. Place tobacco stamps on temples and forehead. Pull hair real hard several times. Apply fresh sliced potato on temples.

Sore eyes—Wash with salt water.

Toothache—If the tooth is decayed burn out the decayed part with hot wire. Hold hot, salty water in the mouth. Chew the root of a plant called *cardo-santo*.

Appendicitis—Mix corn meal in water and drink it before breakfast. Drink a lot of hot salty cow milk.

Boils—Apply poultices made from pine tree gum, yellow laundry soap, chicken dung or hot cow dung.

Itch—Apply a mixture of sulphur and lard before retiring.

Nose Bleeding—Place cigarette paper between upper lip and gum. Burn a live frog, grind the remains and sprinkle around the nose. Be careful that none of the powder goes in the nose. If it does the bleeding will increase. Burn buffalo hair and inhale. Carry a small flint rock in the pocket at all times.

Bed-wetting—Put a few drops of turpentine in water and drink once or twice per day, especially before retiring. Rub HHH medicine on abdomen.

Burns and scalds—Apply writing ink on burned area. Also a mixture of lard, flour, baking soda and vinegar.

Corns—Soak corns in hot water for a few minutes, withdraw, dry and paint with indelible pencil. Yellow laundry soap also good.

Indigestion—A cooked paste made from flour, water, nutmeg and cinnamon.

Fever Blister—Sprinkle blister with powder made from orange rinds.

Sty—Apply mashed fly to affected part.

Removing poisoned blood from the body—Use ventosas or cupping glasses over the injured tissue.

BIBLIOGRAPHY

BIBLIOGRAPHY

Adams, Herbert B. (Editor), *History, Politics and Education*. Baltimore: The Johns Hopkins Press, 1890.

Adams, James T. (Editor), *Dictionary of American History*. New York: Charles Scribner's Sons, 1940, Vol. III.

Bell, Earl H. "Social Stratification in a Small Community," *Scientific Monthly*, XXXVIII, 1934.

Blackmar, Frank Wilson. *Spanish Institutions of the Southwest*. Baltimore: The Johns Hopkins Press, 1891.

Bloom, Lansing B., and Donnelly, Thomas C. *New Mexico History and Civics*. Albuquerque: The University Press, 1933.

Coan, Charles F. *A History of New Mexico*. New York: The American Historical Society, 1925.

Donaldson, Thomas. *The Public Domain*, House Miscellaneous Document 45th, 47th Congress, 2nd session, XIX. Washington: Government Printing Office, 1884.

Dunham, Harold H. *Government Handout*. Ann Arbor: Edwards Bros., Inc., 1941.

Geddes, Joseph A. *Farm Versus Village Living*. Utah Agricultural Experiment Station Bulletin 249, Logan, 1934.

George, Henry. *Our Land and Land Policy*. New York: Doubleday, Doran and Company, Inc., 1911.

Gregg, Josiah, *Commerce of the Prairies*. Dallas: The Southwest Press (reprint), 1933.

Grisham, Glenn. *El Pueblo* (unpublished). Amarillo: Farm Security Administration, 1939.

House of Representatives, Executive Document 73, 45th Congress, 2nd session. Washington: Government Printing Office, 1878.

Johansen, Sigurd. "The Social Organization of Spanish-American Villages," *The Southwestern Social Science Quarterly*, Vol. XXIII, 1942.

Klein, Julius. *The Mesta: A Study in Spanish Economic History, 1273-1836*. Cambridge: Harvard University Press, 1920.

Kluckhohn, Florence R. *Los Atarquenos*. Cambridge: Harvard University (Ph.D. dissertation), 1940.

Leonard, Olen, and Loomis, C. P. *Culture of a Contemporary Rural Community, El Cerrito, New Mexico*. U.S. Department of Agriculture, Bureau of Agricultural Economics, 1941.

Linton, Ralph. *The Study of Man*. New York: D. Appleton-Century Company, 1936.

Loomis, C. P. *Informal Groupings in a Spanish-American Village* (mimeographed bulletin), U.S. Department of Agriculture, Bureau of Agricultural Economics, 1940.

Loomis, C. P., and Leonard, O. E. *Standards of Living in an Indian-Mexican Village and on a Reclamation Project*. Washington: U.S. Department of Agriculture, 1938.

McBride, G. M. *Chile: Land and Society*. New York: American Geographical Society, Research Series 19, 1936.

MacIver, R. M. *Society, A Textbook of Sociology*. New York: Farrar and Rinehart, Inc., 1937.

Maes, Ernest E. "The World and the People of Cundiyo," *Land Policy Review*, March, 1941.

May, Mark A., and Doob, Leonard W. *Competition and Cooperation.* Social Science Research Council Bulletin 25, New York, 1937.

Menefee, Selden C. *Mexican Migratory Workers of South Texas.* Washington: Work Projects Agency, 1941.

Nelson, Lowry. *A Social Survey of Escalanti, Utah.* Brigham Young University, 1925.

_____. *The Mormon Village: A Study in Social Origins.* Provo: Brigham Young University, 1930.

_____. *Some Social and Economic Features of American Fork, Utah.* Provo: Brigham Young University, 1933.

Oberg, Kalervo. "Cultural Factors and Land-Use Planning in Cuba Valley, New Mexico," *Rural Sociology*, Vol. V, No. 4, Dec., 1940.

Odum, Howard W., and Moore, Harry E. *American Regionalism.* New York: Henry Holt and Company, 1938.

Ogburn, William F., and Nimkoff, Meyer F. *Sociology.* New York: Houghton Mifflin Company, 1940.

Powers, Stephen. *Afoot and Alone.* Hartford: Columbian Book Company, 1872.

Public Survey Office. *The Canyon de San Diego Grant.* Report No. 25, File No. 60, U.S. Department of Interior, General Land Office, Santa Fe, New Mexico.

Public Survey Office. *The Cundiyo Grant.* Report No. 211, File No. 246, U.S. Department of the Interior, General Land Office, Santa Fe, New Mexico.

_____. *The Jacona Grant.* Report No. 92, File No. 168, U.S. Department of the Interior, General Land Office, Santa Fe, New Mexico.

_____. *The La Joya Grant.* Report No. 95, File No. 169, U.S. Department of the Interior, General Land Office, Santa Fe, New Mexico.

_____. *The San Miguel del Bado Grant.* Report No. 119, File No. 49, U.S. Department of the Interior, General Land Office, Santa Fe, New Mexico.

Rowntree, B. S. *Poverty, A Study of Town Life.* New York: Longmans, Green and Company, 1922.

Russell, John C. "State Regionalism in New Mexico," *Social Forces*, XIV, 1937.

Sanchez, George I. *A Study of the Scores of Spanish-Speaking Children on Repeated Tests.* A Master's Thesis, Austin: The University of Texas, 1931.

_____. *Forgotten People.* Albuquerque: University of New Mexico Press, 1940.

Sanderson, Dwight, *Rural Sociology and Rural Social Organization.* New York: John Wiley and Sons, 1942.

San Miguel Rural Council. *A Survey of San Geronimo.* Las Vegas: Highlands University, 1936.

_____. *A Survey of Villanueva.* Las Vegas: Highlands University, 1936.

Sato, Shosuke. *History of the Land Question in the United States.* Johns Hopkins University Studies in Historical and Political Science, Fourth Series, VII-IX, Baltimore, 1886.

Simpson, Eyler N. *The Ejido: Mexico's Way Out.* Chapel Hill: The University of North Carolina Press, 1937.

Skinner, Constance L. *Pioneers of the Old Southwest.* New Haven: Yale University Press, 1921.

Smith, T. Lynn, and Parenton, Vernon J. "Acculturation Among the Louisiana French," *The American Journal of Sociology,* XLIV, 1938.

Smith, T. Lynn. "An Analysis of Rural Social Organization Among the French-speaking People of Southern Louisiana," *Journal of Farm Economics,* XVI, 1939.

_____.*The Population of Louisiana: Its Composition and Changes.* Louisiana Agricultural Experiment Station, Bulletin 293, Baton Rouge, 1937.

_____. *The Sociology of Rural Life.* New York: Harper and Brothers, 1940.

Soil Conservation Service. *Material on the Partido System.* Albuquerque: U.S. Department of Agriculture, 1937.

_____. *Notes on Community Owned Land Grants in New Mexico.* Albuquerque: U.S. Department of Agriculture, 1937.

_____. *San Miguel County Villages.* Albuquerque: U.S. Department of Agriculture, 1938.

_____. *Tewa Basin Study.* Albuquerque: U.S. Department of Agriculture, II, 1939.

_____. *Village Livelihood in the Upper Rio Grande Area.* Albuquerque: U.S. Department of Agriculture Bulletin, 1937.

Sorokin, P. A. *Social Mobility.* New York: Harper and Brothers, 1927.

Sorokin, Pitirim A., Zimmerman, Carle C., and Calpin, C. J. *A Systematic Source Book of Rural Sociology.* Minneapolis: University of Minnesota Press, 1930-32, 3 vols.

Taylor, Carl C. *Rural Sociology.* New York: Harper and Brothers, 1933.

Treat, Payson J. *The National Land System, 1785-1820.* New York: E. B. Treat and Company, 1910.

Twitchell, Ralph E. *Leading Facts of New Mexican History.* Cedar Rapids: Torch Press, 1911-1912, 5 vols.

U.S. Department of Agriculture. *Climate and Man; 1941 Yearbook of Agriculture.* Washington: Government Printing Office, 1941.

Walter, Paul, Jr. *A Study of Isolation and Social Change in Three Spanish-speaking Villages of New Mexico.* A Ph.D. thesis, Stanford University,

Young, Kimball. *An Introductory Sociology.* New York: The American Book Company, 1934.
1938.

PLATES

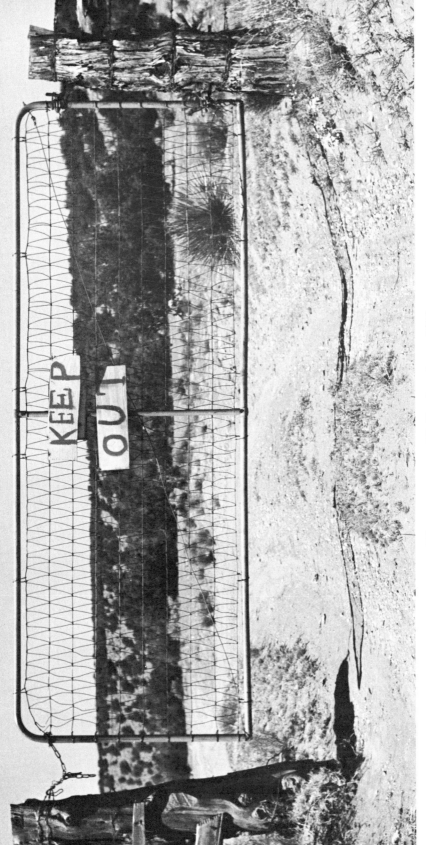

The entrance to El Cerrito, June, 1970.

Louis Aragon, descendant of one of the original grantees.

Estefanita Quintana Aragon, descendant of one of the original grantees.

Three generations of descendants of the Aragon family: father,
son and grandson.

Notices such as this were difficult for the natives to understand.

The Church still stands as a guardian over the village.

El Cerrito Village housing pattern.

El Cerrito today, showing results of surrender.

These ruins indicate several generations of the same family lived here. Page 27 explains the additions to the houses.

Sentinels of a past that is today only a memory.

Reminder of an earlier day.

192

Symbol of a past way of life in El Cerrito.

INDEX

INDEX

Adams, Herbert B., *History, Politics and Education,* 7
Alcalde, 100-101
Amusement, 55, 68-70
Anglos
  area settled, 21
  contacts with Spanish-Americans, 21-22
  date settled, 20-21
  origins, 21
Anton Chico Grant, 106-108

Baile, 30, 68
Blackmar, Frank W., *Spanish Institutions of the Southwest,* 7
Bloom, Lansing B., and Donnelly, Thomas C., *New Mexican History and Civics,* 8

Canyon de San Diego Grant, 110-112
Changes as told by one inhabitant, 50-54
Chili, 32
Church
  Catholic, 70
  definition of, 146
  education, 147
  influence of, 55, 70
  services, 71
  sponsored activities, 72-74
  support of, 72
Clothing, 89
Coan, Charles F., *A History of New Mexico,* 8
Colonization policy of Spanish and Mexicans, 96-103
Corn
  description and use, 32
  Indian, 32
Court of Private Land Claims
  creation of, 103
  deeds and boundary problems, 117
  effects of decision of 1904, 49, 138
  San Miguel del Bado claim reduced, 105

Crops
  dry land, 17, 47-48
  irrigable land, 17, 48
  types grown, 17, 48
Culture
  Mexican, 38
  Spanish-American, 38

Dances, 30, 56, 68-70, 74
Day's labor, 65-66
Decrees
  Mexican
    petition for grazing land, 98
    subsidizing settlers, 100
    territory open to foreigners, 99
  Spanish
    disposition public lands, 97
    petition for *realango* lands, 97
    territory open to foreigners, 99
Donaldson, Thomas, *The Public Domain,* 6
Dunham, Harold H., *Government Handout,* 7

Economy
  early settlement, 40, 47-50
  in 1940, 87-89
Education
  by early Church, 147
  early days, 54
  girls compared to boys, 81-82
  parents interest in, 82-83
  teaching techniques, 84
El Cerrito
  accommodation, assimilation, and acculturation, 136-139
  agriculture techniques, 60-63
  amusements, 55, 68-70
  choice of, 41
  climate, 46-47
  competition, conflict and cooperation, 131-136
  description of, 43-45
  economy, 47
  history and background, 45-56
  interviews, 3-5
  land
    loss of, 48-49, 105, 150
    ownership of, 56-58, 153

195